| | |
|---|---|
| COPYRIGHT NOTICE...................... | |
| POTTED HISTORY........................... | |
| ROMEO AND JULIET ...................... | |
| FAMOUS LOCALS............................ | ..................... 8 |
| GET READY ................................................................ 9 | |
| THE MAPS ................................................................ 11 | |
| THE WALKS............................................................... 12 | |
| WALK 1 – AROUND THE ARENA............................... 13 | |
| WALK 2 – SCALIGERS AND DANTE ........................... 32 | |
| WALK 3 – THE CHURCHES AND BRIDGES .................. 75 | |
| WALK 4 – PALACES AND THE MUSEUM................... 121 | |
| WALK 5 – ACROSS THE RIVER ................................ 155 | |
| WALK 6 - JULIET'S TOMB? ..................................... 168 | |
| DID YOU ENJOY THESE WALKS?.............................. 181 | |
| OTHER STROLLING AROUND BOOKS TO TRY: ......... 182 | |

# Copyright Notice

**Strolling Around Verona by Irene Reid**

ISBN: 9781709369537

All rights reserved. This book may not be reproduced in any form, in whole or in part, without written permission from the author.

The author has made every effort to ensure the accuracy of the information in this book at the time of going to press, and cannot accept responsibility for any consequences arising from the use of the book.

*Many thanks to John and Diane
who tirelessly checked these walks while in Verona*

# Potted History

The first settlers in this area built on the banks of the river Adige because the river crossed a fertile plain – an ideal location for a new settlement.

## The Romans

The little town of Verona was later colonised by Rome, and Verona rapidly became a very important city because several of Rome's major roads were directed through the city – especially the important Via Postumia which ran across the top of Italy. The roads opened the way for trade and Verona became an important communication hub with links to both the Adriatic and all the surrounding states. Unfortunately it also provided a handy road for invaders – making Verona an easy target when the Roman Empire fell.

## Invasions

The invaders always came from the north, first the Goths arrived in the sixth century, then the Lombards, and the Franks headed by Charlemagne – each taking a turn in ruling the city.

The most notorious ruler of these times was Ezzelino da Romano III who ruled in the thirteenth century. He is thought to have been the most vicious and cruellest tyrant ever to rule northern Italy.

He is reputed to have committed many atrocities, e.g. he had 11,000 citizens of nearby Padua burned to death, and on another occasion he had the eyes, noses and legs removed from the population of the town Friola.

He ruled for 33 years, and the people of the time thought he was the son of the devil. He was excommunicated twice and finally Pope Innocent IV mounted a crusade against him. His many enemies stood together and finally he was defeated. To avoid capture he killed himself. The poet Dante placed him in that part of hell reserved for:

> "Tyrants who delighted in blood
> and gave themselves thereto."

Verona finally became an independent city in the 13th century. Italy, the country as we know it today, just didn't exist. Instead each city was an autonomous state, and spent much of its time fighting and trying to invade other cities.

## The Scaliger Family

It was at this time that the Scaliger family rose to power in Verona. As you explore you will see them referred to as the Scaliger, Scaligeri, or della Scala family. It's a little confusing but they are all the same family.

Mastino della Scala was the first to wield real power when he became the "Podesta", the city's chief Judge. Mastino's real name was Leonardo, but he was given the nickname Mastino which means mastiff, a breed of dog used for hunting and war, which perhaps gives us a clue to his nature. He was later elected as Captain of the city for life, and he turned it into a heredity title to ensure someone in his family was always the ruler of Verona. His family ruled the city successfully for over a century afterwards.

The Scaliger era was seen as a golden time for Verona as the city became very rich and important. However despite conferring peace and prosperity on the city, the Scaligers themselves were not a peaceful crew. The family had a propensity to kill each other off to gain power. Brother killed brother, nephew killed uncle, no holds barred. The most famous members of the family were Cangrande I, Cansignorio, and Cangrande II. You will read those names many times as you explore Verona and see the buildings and monuments they added during their reign.

Cangrande I was actually christened Can Francesco, but he was nicknamed Cangrande which translates as "Big Dog" because of his warlike personality – continuing the canine obsession by the family. The name stuck, and the dog motif was adopted enthusiastically by the rest of the family. They even placed the image of an angry dog on their helmets and tombs.

The Scaligers finally lost control of Verona when the city fell to The Duke of Milan, Gian Galeazzo, in the fourteenth century. Galeazzo had already seized the reins of power in Milan and he quickly took control of the rest of Northern Italy. He later died of the plague and his much less competent son soon lost his father's empire. However Verona didn't regain its independence, because Venice saw the opportunity and took over Northern Italy instead.

## Venetian Rule

Verona lived in peace and prosperity under Venetian rule, and not much happened until Napoleon arrived in 1797. He invaded Northern Italy as part of the battle against Austria.

Control of Verona and the rest of Northern Italy then switched back and forth between Napoleon and the Austro-Hungarian Empire until Napoleon was finally defeated seventeen years later.

## Austrian Rule

The Austrians then ruled, but the idea of Italy as a country had taken hold.

Garibaldi and the future King Victor Emmanuel II started to build Italy, state by state, city by city. Verona finally joined the new Kingdom of Italy in 1866 and Austria left the scene.

## World War II

Mussolini's Italy was allied with Germany in World War II, but after a few years Mussolini lost power and Italy switched sides to join the allies. Germany promptly took control of Italy.

Verona became the transport hub of Italy's Jews as they were transported north to the concentration camps.

Sadly by the end of the war, 40% of the city had been destroyed including all the bridges over the river Adige.

## European Market

Italy joined the European Market and in 2000 the ancient city of Verona became a World Heritage Site.

# Romeo and Juliet

A large part of Verona's tourist industry is formed around Shakespeare's tragic tale of Romeo and Juliet. If you have never read it at school or seen it in a film, here is an abridged version:

The Montague family and the Capulet family hate each other.

Romeo M has his eye on pretty Rosaline who happens to be going to a party at the Capulets' house. Romeo and his mates gate-crash the party so that Romeo can chat up Rosaline. Meanwhile Juliet C has been told that the very eligible Paris likes her and she plans to check him out the party.

Things don't go to plan. Romeo and Juliet meet at the party and fall instantly in love. They realise that their parents are going to be less than happy about it, so they get married the next day in secret.

That same day Benvolio M meets Tybalt C and they start fighting. Romeo and his best friend Mercutio get dragged into the argument. Tybalt kills Mercutio, so Romeo kills Tybalt. Romeo is banished from Verona by the Prince, who had already warned both families that he was sick of their constant fighting.

The friar who married the lovers tries to persuade the Prince into letting Romeo off. Meanwhile Juliet's dad, who doesn't know his daughter is already hitched, agrees to let Paris marry her. Juliet is distraught and threatens to kill herself, so the friar suggests she takes a knockout potion instead as it will make her seem dead. Juliet thinks that's a great plan, takes the potion, is declared dead, and is placed in the Capulet family tomb. The plan is that Romeo will return to her grave and wake her up, however the message with that vital information never got to Romeo. So he races back to Juliet's tomb, drinks some handy poison to be with her, and drops dead.

Juliet wakes up to find Romeo dead and stabs herself with a dagger in grief. Everyone arrives at the tomb to find the dead lovers, and agree that they really should stop arguing before anyone else gets hurt.

# Famous Locals

## Veronese

Verona's most successful artist was Paolo Caliari who adopted the name of his home city to become Veronese.

He worked mostly in Venice and Verona, and Verona has only a few of his masterpieces. He is renowned for large dramatic scenes, and you will see one of his major works as you explore.

# Get Ready

## The Opera

If you are keen on opera and are visiting during the summer opera season, you might want to purchase tickets for the Arena. You can buy them on-line or at the tourist office near the Arena.

Many of the most well-known operas are staged with extravagant scenery and performances. There is a wide range of ticket prices, so you can throw caution to the winds and make it a special night, or go for the cheapest seats just to see the show.

Warning 1 – Unless you buy the most expensive seats don't expect an evening of comfort. Most people sensibly hire a cushion as they enter the Arena to make it a less painful experience, as the operas do last for several hours. However it is quite a spectacle and well worth doing.

Warning 2 – The opera doesn't stop if it rains until the first Act is over. To do so would mean refunding the audience, so the opera will continue until Act 1 is completed. Be prepared and take some sort of rain protection with you to pull on should the heavens open.

## Corte Sgarzarie Cryptoporticus

You can visit the Cryptoporticus - an underground Roman ruin which you will pass by on Walk 2 – see Underground Verona on Page 44.

However, you need to plan ahead to get access. If you are interested you can find information on how to visit here:

https://www.archeonaute.it/corte-sgarzerie/#sgarzerie

## Tourist Office

The Tourist Office is the best place to go to purchase a sightseeing card as explained below. You can also pick up a free city map. Another useful item is a bus map which you will need if you plan to use the buses to reach any of the further out sights. Walk 3 which takes you to the four major churches does recommend using a bus to reach the final church.

You can find the Tourist Office near Piazza Bra, which is convenient as that is where Walk 1 starts. When you get to the Piazza you will see the impressive town wall on the opposite side of the square from the Arena. The tourist office is built into the wall at Via degli Alpini 9.

## Tourist Card

Verona offers two types of pass for tourists.

### Verona Card

The biggest and most expensive is the Verona Card which gets you into most of the major sights, and which you can buy to cover 1 or 2 days.

The web site states you can buy the card at any of the included sights, but when put into practice the smaller locations only stock the single day cards. So your best option is to buy your card from either the tourist office or at one of the major sights such as the Arena.

Details can be found here:

https://www.verona-tickets.com/attractions-in-verona/city-card/

### Churches Card

There is another card which can be bought at one of the four major churches:

- The Cathedral
- Santa Anastasia
- San Zeno
- San Fermo

It only gives you entrance to the four churches. So if your plan is to visit the churches and give the Arena and the Museums a miss, you would be better buying this card.

The only down side is that it lasts just one day, so you would have to visit them all on the same day. Three are reasonably close to each other, but the church of San Zeno would probably require using the bus system to reach it.

Details can be found here:

https://www.chieseverona.it/en/visit-info

## The Maps

There are maps sprinkled all through the walks to help you find your way. If you need to check where you are at any point during a walk, always flip back to find the map you need.

To help you follow the maps, each map shows its start point. In addition numbered directions have been placed on each map. The numbers correspond to the directions within the walks.

# The Walks

There are 5 walks for you to enjoy:

## Walk 1 - Around the Arena (1.5 km)

Explore around Piazza Bra and visit the famous Arena.

## Walk 2 – Scaligers and Dante (1.5 km)

See Juliet's House before walking around Piazza delle Erbe and then into Piazza Signori.

Note - this walk includes the Corte Sgarzarie where you have a chance to descend into Verona's Roman past. So plan accordingly.

## Walk 3 – The Churches (1.5 km + Bus)

Visit Verona's four major churches.

## Walk 4 – Mansions and the Museum (2.1km)

Walk from Piazza Bra to the Castelvecchio museum and back again.

## Walk 5 – Across the River (2 km)

Cross the river to the Roman Theatre, then along the riverbank before re-crossing the river to the Cathedral.

## Walk 6 – Juliet's Tomb (2 km)

Walk to Juliet's Tomb which lies outside the old city wall.

# Walk 1 – Around the Arena

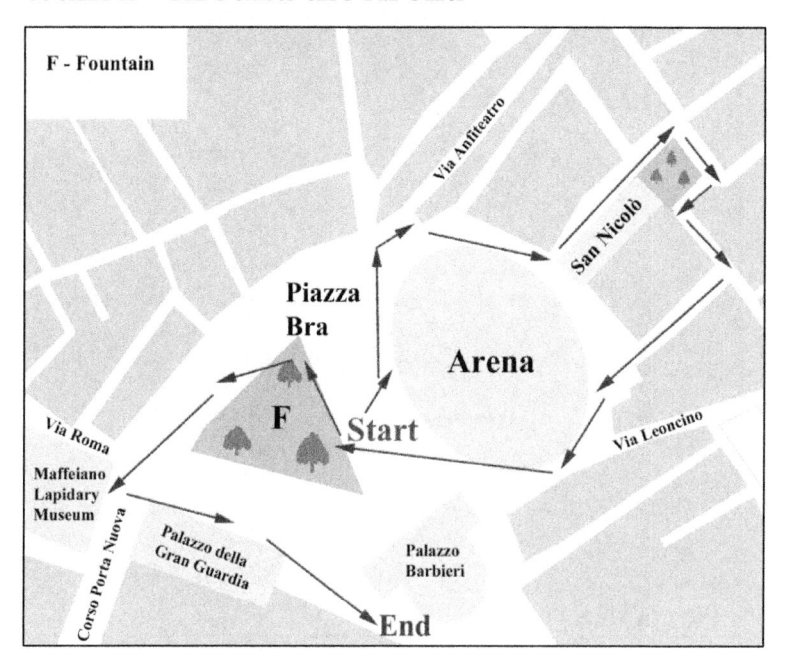

Overview Walk 1

This walk takes you around Piazza Bra, the large square which is home to the Arena.

As you might expect the Arena is always busy, so try to start just before Arena opening time to give yourself a chance of beating the crowds.

At the time of writing the Arena opens at 9:00 am, but it's best to check on its website before you set out:

https://verona.com/en/verona/arena-di-verona/

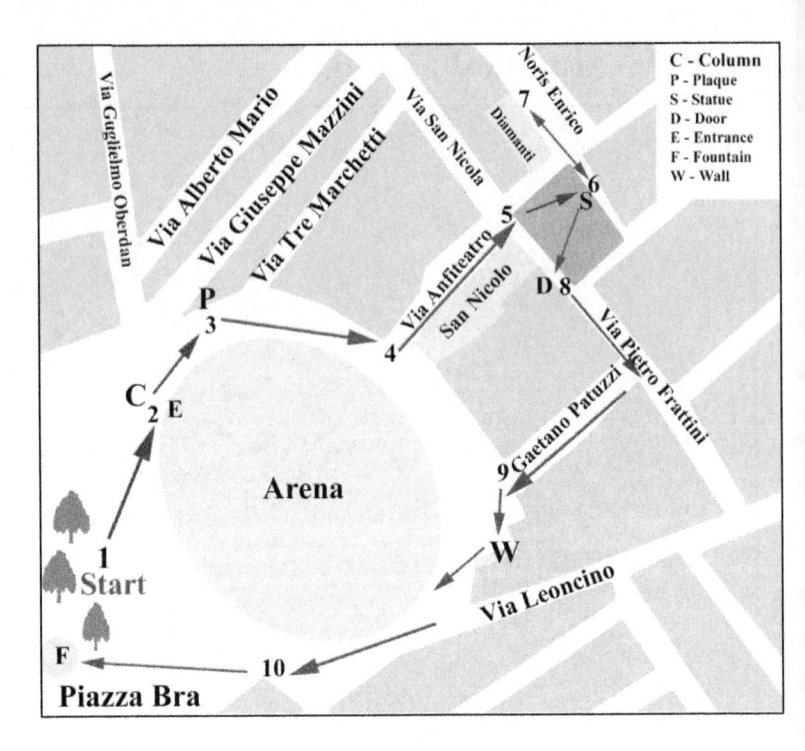

Map 1

## Piazza Bra

The square's odd name is thought to come from the German word "breit" which means broad, which the square certainly is.

*Map 1.1 – Head for the entrance to get into the Arena. To find it, stand with the tree-filled garden behind you and face the arena.*

*At the time of writing, the tourist entrance is on the left hand side of the arena. If you have bought a Verona Card, you don't have to queue at the ticket desk. There is a second desk further in where you can get your Verona card checked. So just head in.*

## The Arena

Even if you have tickets to see a show in the evening, it's worth going in during the day just to wander all over the seating area, and to imagine the gladiators fighting to the death below you. You can carefully climb up to the higher seats, sit in the sunshine, and just take it all in.

**The Romans**

As you know from the potted history, Verona became a very important Roman city, and like all important Roman cities it had an amphitheatre. The Romans built this one in the 1st century AD and it's the third largest they ever built, only beaten by Rome's Coliseum and another theatre in Capua.

Its purpose was to stage shows and games to keep the population happy. A maze of tunnels beneath the amphitheatre was used by hundreds of slaves to move props, animals, and people into position for the show.

At first the Arena staged shows with rare and exotic beasts being slaughtered. Pliny, who recorded much of the history of the Roman Empire, records that a citizen called Maximus funded several entertainments in honour of his dead wife. One of his special evenings was a bit of a let-down, because the ship bringing some panthers from Africa got held up by a storm.

Tastes changed and the entertainment got more blood-thirsty. First slaves were killed instead of animals, then Christians, and finally the gladiators had to battle each other. As you try to imagine the gladiatorial battles, remember that life as a gladiator was brutal and tended to be short.

**After the Romans**

When the Roman Empire fell the amphitheatre was quarried extensively, and it's amazing that it has survived as intact as it has, although it has lost its top tier. The outer wall was faced with pretty pink and white limestone, but after a huge earthquake in the twelfth century it collapsed. The fallen stones became a convenient quarry for material to construct other buildings, so today we have just the bare wall left. If you visit the Castelvecchio on walk 3 you might spot some of the huge stone blocks which were dragged from the Arena to build it.

The Arena was used many times over the centuries to stage all kinds of shows, although none as blood-thirsty as those the Romans loved.

Antonio della Scala laid on a show at the arena in the fifteenth century to whitewash the fratricide of his brother Bartolomeo. Bartolomeo was very popular with the people and Antonio wanted rid of him. So he had him assassinated and then tried to have the family of Bartolomeo's fiancée framed for his murder. The people did not believe that story and Antonio's public standing plummeted. So he laid on a hugely extravagant show in the Arena, and invited the city to celebrate his own betrothal. The city partied for 27 days and conveniently forgot about the crimes.

**Napolean**

There is an interesting story about Napoleon and the Arena. He requested that a traditional bull-fight be staged when he was in power. Such events were quite different from Spanish bullfights; a mastiff fighting dog was let loose in the Arena to bring the bull down.

On the big night a particularly wild bull was in the Arena, and one by one the poor dogs were gored to death. Napoleon lost patience and ordered that two dogs were used – they died. Napoleon demanded three were used - they died. Finally he ordered that all the remaining dogs were let loose, and the poor bull was bitten and dragged down to its death.

It's said that Napoleon was advised by a friend to remember what had happened to the bull, pointing out that Napoleon could defeat his enemies one by one, but if they joined forces he was doomed. Napoleon clearly didn't learn the lesson and of course he was defeated when Europe united against him.

**The Arena today**

In the early twentieth century Buffalo Bill's Wild West Show put on a show in the Arena to packed houses, and even today it draws the crowds to see shows from rock concerts to the annual opera festival.

***When you are ready to move on, exit the Arena and turn right.***

## Around the Arena

As you do, you will see the only surviving section of the arena's third level of arches rising above you on your right. There is also a pretty devotional column near the Arena entrance.

Stand beside the column and look along Via Giuseppe Mazzini, which is a marble paved street. You can see the tall Torre dei Lamberti way in the distance – you will get a chance to climb it in on Walk 2.

Via Giuseppe Mazzini was built to join Verona's two most important piazzas, Piazza Bra and Piazza delle Erbe, and it's named after Giuseppe Mazzini, a politician and journalist who was a key figure in bringing about a united Italy.

*Map 1.2 – Walk beyond the devotional column towards the first right-hand building of Via Giuseppe Mazzini. You will find a plaque commemorating Carlotta Aschieri.*

# Carlotta Aschieri

> IN QUESTA CASA
> CARLOTTA ASCHIERI
> VENTICINQUENNE E INCINTA
> CADDE TRUCIDATA DAGLI AUSTRIACI
> ULTIMO SFOGO
> DI MORIBONDA TIRANNIDE
> 6 OTTOBRE 1866

In this house Carlotta Aschieri,
twenty-five and pregnant,
was killed by the Austrians,
the last outlet of a dying tyranny

As the Italian wars of unification drew to a close, the Austrian-Hungarian army was less than happy at being ousted from Northern Italy.

While peace negotiations proceeded towards an end to hostilities, Verona's civilians happily celebrated and people were out on the streets waving the Italian flag. Some Austrian soldiers started to pick fights with them, and Carlotta was stabbed with a bayonet and killed. Carlotta was aged just twenty-five and seven months pregnant. Just ten days later the Veneto joined the newly unified Italy and Austria departed.

*Map 1.3 - Continue around the arena passing narrow Via Tre Marchetti on your left.*

*Map 1.4 - Turn left down the next street, Via Anfiteatro - the old building on your right as you do is the San Nicolò all'Arena church. Walk to the end of the church and turn right into Piazza San Nicolò.*

# Piazza San Nicolò

This is a nice little square which has recently been renovated by The Angels of Beauty, a group of volunteers who aim to take care of the parks, gardens, and monuments of Verona.

In the middle is a modern statue called "Fruit Object Sculpture" - it's up to you which fruit you think the sculptor was aiming for.

It was donated by the heirs of the sculptor Gino Bogoni, who was a local artist. He wrote the following about his fruit sculpture in his papers just before entering hospital:

> "This could well be my last work; I cannot risk it remaining at the stage of an idea or even of a sketch. I absolutely must bring it to completion first, at whatever cost. And here it is at last, completed".

He died shortly after.

***Map 1.5 - Walk across the square to stand behind the "fruit" to get the best view of the church.***

## San Nicolò all'Arena

The church is built on the site of a much older church also dedicated to Saint Nicholas. It was knocked down in the seventeenth century to build this one, but because of the plague and lack of funds the new church was never quite completed – it lacked a dome, a bell-tower, and even a façade.

In the end, the missing dome was just quietly forgotten about and the roof was finally sealed at much less expense. The façade got added after World War II when the builders made use of the stones from other destroyed buildings. As for the bell-tower, the people of Verona decided they didn't want anything towering over the Arena, so that idea was also just put aside.

If it's open, go in to see where the dome should have been, and its trompe l'oeil replacement. The church did have frescoes at one time but they are now squirreled away in the Castelvecchio museum – so you might see them if you visit it on walk 4.

*Return to the "fruit" and face the church once more.*

*Map 1.6 - Turn right and walk to the end of the square and into Via Noris Enrico. The Palazzo di Diamanti sits on your left-hand side.*

## Palazzo dei Diamanti

It's pretty obvious how it got its name. It was built by the wealthy Cappella family in the fifteenth century

It was partially destroyed by allied bombing but has been lovingly recreated, including its beautiful balcony and ornate door, so take a few steps to see it.

The door is topped by two lovely angels on either side of a man's head. Above them is a memorial stone which records the year the building was damaged, 1944, and when it was restored, 1950.

*Map 1.7 - Return to "The Fruit" and face the church once more. Walk diagonally left to cross the square.*

At the corner of the square stands a building attached to the church. It has a very ancient door which is accompanied by some equally elderly windows.

*Map 1.8 - Facing that old door, turn left along Via Pietro Frattini, and then take the next right into Via Leone Gaetano Patuzzi.*

*As you reach the Arena look left to find the Mura Gallieno.*

## Mura Gallieno

Old Verona sits in a loop of the river Adige, and it was protected by the river on the north, east, and west sides.

The first town wall ran east to west, to close the river loop and give the town vital protection from the south. At that time, this area including the Arena lay outside the wall.

By the third century the barbarians were invading Italy from Northern Europe. Emperor Gallienus decided to replace the existing wall and had the new bigger and stronger wall erected in record time. While he was at it, he had it expanded to enclose the Arena area. Here you can see a remnant of that city wall expansion

*Map 1.9 – Facing the Arena, turn left to follow the arena wall.*

*Map 1.10 - Make your way to the centre of Piazza Bra once more. Stand by the fountain in the middle of the tree-filled garden.*

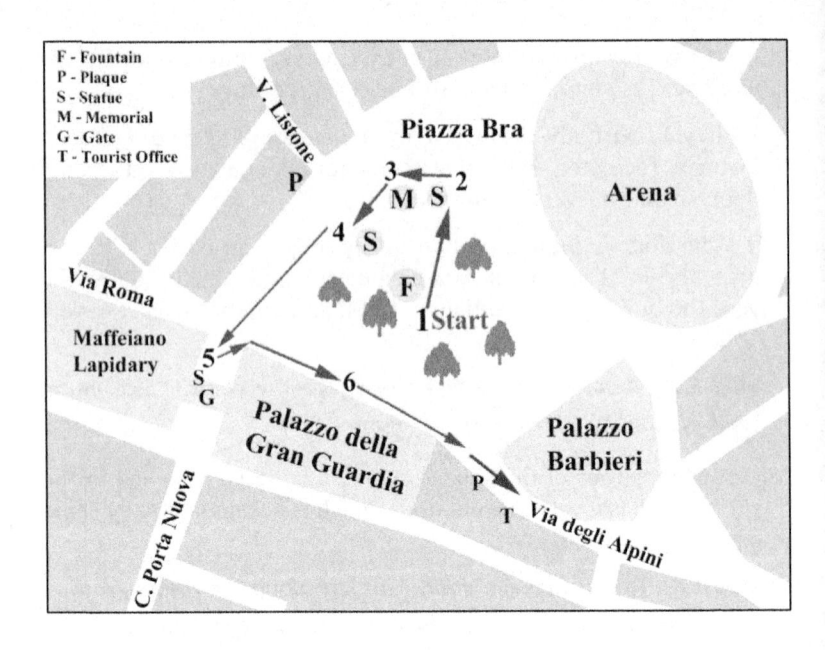

Map 2

## The Lemon Squeezer

This fountain is officially called "The fountain of the Alps".

The locals prefer to call it the "lemon squeezer", because they think that's what it looks like. It was given by Germany when Verona was twinned with Munich. Munich got a lovely statue of Juliet in return, and she now stands near Munich town hall, so figure out which city got the best deal.

***Map 2.1 - Stand facing the fountain with the Arena behind you. Follow the path through the trees on your right-hand side and you will reach a statue.***

# Caduti per la liberta

This young man represents the Partisans of Italy. While fascist Mussolini was in power, Italy was allied with Germany. When Mussolini was brought down Italy switched to support the allies, but of course Germany immediately took control of the country and put a puppet government in place.

The Partisans fought against the Italian puppet government until the end of World War II. The statue was erected in 1946 one year after the end of the war.

Some have compared it to Michelangelo's David which stands in Florence. The figure is certainly standing in a similar pose but with a few more clothes.

***Map 2.2 - Stand face-to-face with the statue and turn right to walk around the park a little. You will find a war memorial on the lawn on your left after a few steps.***

## War Memorial

Italy's treatment of the Jews during World War II was very inconsistent. Officially Italy followed the German policy of persecuting Jews from the onset of the war, with confiscation of property and segregation. Unofficially the authorities chose to ignore many of the new laws.

Later, when Italy switched sides and was occupied by Germany, the laws were enforced with Nazi efficiency. Some Italians saved their Jewish friends and neighbours, hiding them and saving them from transportation to the camps. However others were not so fortunate; this memorial commemorates the Italians who died in German concentration camps, and lists the camp names.

*Map 2.3 - A little further on stands an equestrian statue.*

## King Victor Emmanuel II

It is King Victor Emmanuel II, the first king of a United Italy. Until 1870 Italy did not exist as one country; the northern parts were ruled by the Austria-Hungarian Empire, The Pope ruled the central area as The Papal States, and the remainder were a group of independent city states. Italian unification took sixty years and a series of wars fought all over the country.

Victor Emmanuel became King of Sardinia when his father stepped down having been defeated in the first Italian War of Independence. Victor Emmanuel I had tried to take control of Northern Italy which was ruled by the Austrians – and he had failed. His son therefore became Victor Emmanuel II and made peace with the Austrian-Hungarian Empire.

Ten years later he allied with France and the second war of independence began, as together they battled the Austrians. When that war ended most of Northern Italy was under the Italian crown, but you might wonder what happened to the rest of Italy? King Emmanuel II is facing a balcony which has a plaque above it. It bears the words:

Roma O Morte<br>
Rome or Die

in large letters.

## Garibaldi

Garibaldi was a maverick who dreamt of a united Italy. He led an army from Sicily which crossed over into the independent Kingdom of Naples during the Wars of Independence. They soon had the south of Italy under control and ceded it to King Emmanuel II to bring Italy together.

However The Papal States in the middle were still independent. General Garibaldi demanded that the battle continue to unite ALL of Italy. That balcony is where he told the people of Verona that his army was heading for Rome. The people in Piazza Bra replied with Garibaldi's famous war-cry "Roma O Morte".

Eventually the Papal States were seized and the Pope was left with only The Vatican. Italy was finally one country with Victor Emmanuel II as its king.

King Victor Emmanuel II is known as Padre della patria, Father of the Fatherland, and most Italian cities have a statue of him somewhere, but most also have a statue to General Garibaldi who was just as important.

***Map 2.4 - Now stand face to face with Victor Emmanuel. Turn right and you will see a crenelated double archway at the corner of the square. That is the Portoni della Bra. Make your way over to it.***

## Portoni della Brà

The old Roman town wall was replaced by this much more substantial wall of sturdy brick. It was built by the ruling Scaliger family sometime in the thirteenth century.

The gate you see in front of you is made of much more decorative marble. It replaced the smaller single arch gate which originally stood here, and was inserted into the wall by the Duke of Milan during his short reign in the fourteenth century.

### Step through the archway

Look to your left to see the Pentagonal Tower. It gave the army a means of guarding the gateway, and of keeping an eye on arrivals from the South.

*Return through the archway to find the bust of Shakespeare and a plaque which sit on one side of the gate.*

## Shakespeare bust

The bust of Shakespeare is by Sergio Pasetto, a sculptor from near Verona. It was bought by the "Club of Juliet" and given to Verona. You will see more of Pasetto's works as you explore.

In Shakespeare's tragic love story, Romeo kills Tybalt and then has to leave Verona or face the consequences. He considers this banishment worse than death, because he cannot bear to live knowing he will never see Juliet again.

A plaque sits on city gate, as it is where Romeo left Verona to travel to Mantua. It bears Romeo's despairing words:

> There is no world without Verona walls,
> But purgatory, torture, hell itself.
> Hence-banished is banish'd from the world,
> And world's exile is death: then banished

*Facing Shakespeare, find the door on your right which is the entrance to the Maffeiano Lapidary Museum.*

## Maffeiano Lapidary Museum

Verona had one of the oldest Philharmonic Academies in Europe, dating from the sixteenth century. By the early eighteenth century some of its members decided it was high time that Verona had a proper theatre and opera house.

Step up Scipione Maffei. He convinced his colleagues to fund a huge project to build both a theatre and a museum, and this is the result.

If you have time, you could visit the Museum and also see the courtyard of the theatre.

### The Museum

The museum is one of Europe's oldest archaeological museums, full of Roman, Greek, and Etruscan stones and monuments.

The core of the collection was gathered by Scipione Maffei who was fascinated by antiquities. He gathered together ancient inscriptions and stones found in Verona and surrounding areas.

Some of the collection is placed in the courtyard of the Philharmonic Theatre which is fronted by six huge ionic columns. Inside the museum you can see much more, and if you venture to the upper floor you can enjoy a great view of Piazza Bra and the Arena.

Napoleon stole many of the exhibits during his time as ruler - a lot of them have been returned, but The Louvre holds onto the rest.

**Philharmonic Theatre**

When Mozart and his father visited Verona in 1770 they planned to exhibit Mozart's talents at the theatre, but it took a week before the Academy could slot him into their busy schedule. However when they did, the Academy was astounded at Mozart's ability and offered him membership of the Academy just one year later.

After that concert Mozart's father wrote to his wife and mentioned that they had visited both the Arena and the Lapidary Museum – so you are following in Mozart's footsteps.

*Map 2.5 – With the Lapidary Museum door behind you, the building directly in front of you is the side of the Palazzo della Gran Gauria.*

*Cross the road in front of you, then turn left to walk round the corner of the Palazzo. Climb the steps and walk along the front of the Palazzo. Pause about half-way along the front.*

## Palazzo della Gran Guardia

The Palazzo sits on what was once the southern boundary of Verona, with the city wall bounding it on both sides.

In the seventeenth century Verona was ruled by Venice. Captain Giovanni Mocenigo sent a request to the Doge of Venice, asking for somewhere his troops could exercise and parade out of the rain. The Doge obliged and building started way back in 1610.

However it took over two hundred years to finally complete it because they ran out of money. By the time the palazzo was finished, Piazza Bra had been cleared of hundreds of years of debris. The result was that the new palazzo was left sitting a few meters above the street. So they built the wide flight of steps you see in front of you now.

The thirteen arches along the façade mirror the arches on the Roman Arena.

These days the palazzo is mostly used for exhibitions and private functions, and is not open to the public.

*With the palazzo behind you, the large many-columned building which sits to your right is the Palazzo Barbieri.*

## Palazzo Barbieri

This was where the bureaucrats worked when Verona was ruled by the Austro-Hungarian Empire, and it was named after its architect. These days it is the town hall.

It does have a wonderful tapestry room, but unless you get an invitation to a wedding you won't get a chance to see it. You may however at least see a wedding party on the steps, as it is a very popular venue.

*Map 2.6 - Continue along the front of the Palazzo della Gran Guardia. When you reach its end you will see the turreted city wall on your right. It runs from the arena for some distance.*

## Verona's walls

You saw a remnant of Verona's Roman wall near the Arena earlier, but this huge castellated wall is not part of it. It was built much later in the twelfth century, when Verona was a self-governing city.

The wall was then added to and modified over the centuries by the various rulers of Verona.

The wall forms a loop around Verona. It runs east from here to cross the river. It then runs north, then west across the hills behind Verona, before turning south again and finally re-crossing the river from the west.

*Just a few steps along the wall will bring you to a large memorial which is bordered by greenery. It commemorates the 6th Alpini Regiment.*

## 6th Alpini Regiment

Benito Mussolini was desperate for Italy to join what he saw as the real fighting in WWII, but Hitler and his generals didn't really have much faith in the Italian army as it had already been defeated several times.

Hitler would have preferred that the Italian army stay in the Mediterranean area to keep the British army busy. Finally though, Germany agreed that an Italian army should join the attack on Russia. So the soldiers from sunny Italy headed north into the snows of Russia.

It was a disaster for the Axis powers. The Italians were hopelessly outgunned and unprepared for fighting in the frozen north, but so to their shock were the Germans. One German division was pinned down in Nikolayevka and surrounded by the Soviet troops. To the Germans' astonishment, the remnants of the Italian army, led by the 6th Alpini Regiment, battled against huge odds to break the siege and let the surviving German soldiers escape. The regiment was awarded several medals for bravery and this commemorates their fallen.

Note, if you haven't visited the tourist office yet, now is your chance as it's just a few doors further along the wall.

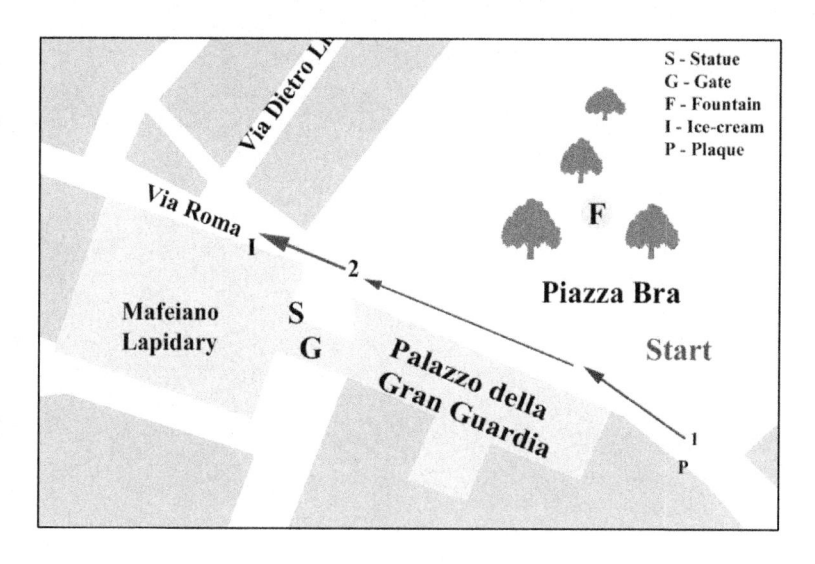

Map 3

## Ice Cream

If an ice-cream appeals to you there is a very good gelateria nearby. There is often a queue as it's very popular.

*Map 3.1 - Make your way back along the front of the Palazzo della Gran Guardia.*

*Map 3.2 – With the Portini della Bra on your left, walk straight ahead into Via Roma.*

*Stay on the left-hand side of Via Roma and just a few steps along will bring you to Gelateria Savoia which sits behind some columns.*

You have now reached the end of this walk.

# Walk 2 – Scaligers and Dante

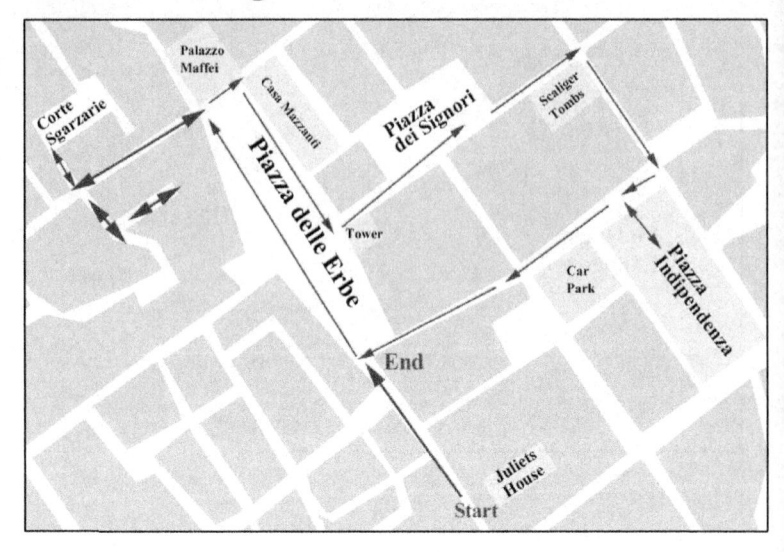

Overview Walk 2

This walk takes you around the oldest part of Verona, visiting Juliet's House, then to Piazza delle Erbe and Piazza dei Signori which are both packed with history.

Finally you visit the fascinating Scaliger Tombs before strolling back to Piazza delle Erbe.

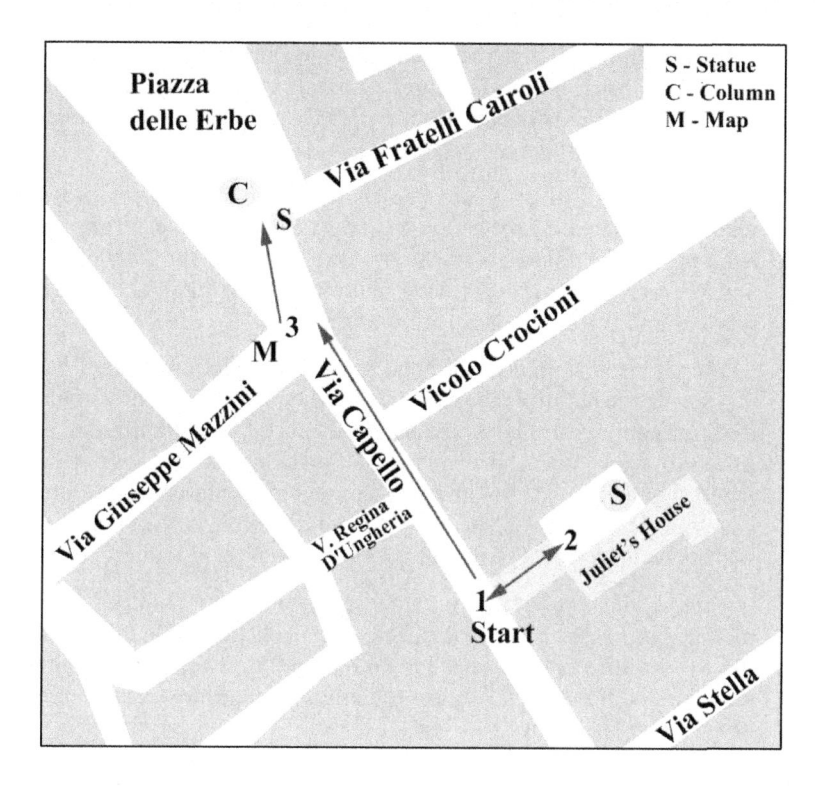

Map 1

Start at Juliet's House, which sits in Via Cappello at number 23. It's quite near Piazza delle Erbe.

Juliet's House is one of the most crowded spots in Verona, so try to get there for opening time to avoid the worst of the crush.

At the time of writing, it opens at 8:30 except on Sundays when its 13:30.

## Juliet's House

Go through the archway and along a short passageway. Due to the number of tourists you might have to shuffle along to see it.

A local tradition tells us that if lovers leave a note on the passageway wall with their names on it, their love will last for eternity.

The result was that this wall was soon plastered with sticky notes, and it started to look awful and damage the brickwork. So love notes on the walls are now strictly banned and if you attach one you get a hefty fine.

Verona has put up some boards as a replacement for those who can't bear to miss the chance of declaring their love. There is even a team of volunteers who try to answer all the love notes and letters. There was a movie made about it called "Letters to Juliet" – and the team work from Juliet's house

The house originally belonged to the Cappello family and you can see their coat of arms inside the courtyard. That family name is quite similar to Shakespeare's fictional Capulet family name. Antonia Avena was the director of museums in the 1900's, so when this house was bought to become a museum he decided to use that similarity to turn it into Juliet's House. An ancient balcony was attached to the house and a legend was made.

In the courtyard stands a lovely statue of Juliet. Tradition tells us that if you touch her right breast you will find your own true love. So far the authorities have not banned that activity but they have moved the original statue to a museum and the one you see now is a replacement.

If you go into the house itself you can see many items which are from the time of Romeo and Juliet. Enjoy immersing yourself in the romantic story but remember, it's just a story.

***Map 1.2 - Exit back onto Via Cappella and turn right.***

***Pass little Vicolo Regina d'Ungheria on your left and Vicolo Crocioni on your right. You will reach a much larger street on your left, Via Giuseppe Mazzini.***

## Via Giuseppe Mazzini

This is the other end of the marbled street you saw on Walk 1 - it runs from Piazza Bra to Piazza delle Erbe.

Spot the map etched into a slab on the right hand side of the street, it shows you the layout of Verona long ago.

*Map 1.3 - Continue along Via Cappello and a few more steps will bring you to the edge of Piazza delle Erbe. You will see a statue of the poet Barbarani on your right.*

## Berto Barbarani

He came from Verona, although you probably won't have heard of him. He must have written some good poems because the Ministry awarded him an annuity for life in 1940 which meant that he didn't have to worry about making a living. However he died just five years later.

One of his most popular poems starts with the line

> Voria cantar Verona
> I want to sing of Verona

and it goes on to tell the story of Verona and its people.

*Just beyond Barbarani stands a devotional column which is called the Colunna del Mercato.*

## Colonna del Mercato

This gothic column was built in the fourteenth century by the Duke of Milan during the short period that Milan ruled Verona. It was he who conquered Verona and ended the reign of the Scaliger family.

You are now at the southern end of Piazza delle Erbe.

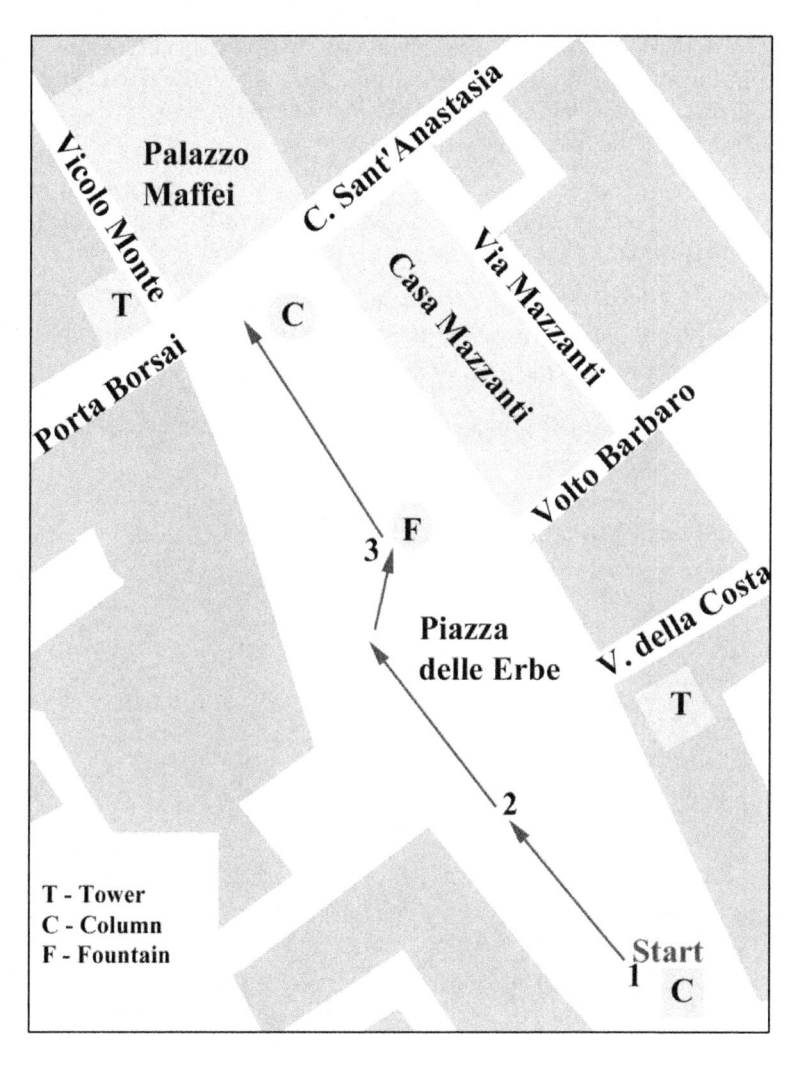

Map 2

## Piazza delle Erbe

It's an oddly elongated square which has a long history.

It's thought to sit on what was the original Roman Forum and was where chariot races took place. Later the piazza became the herb market – hence its current name. There is still a market held in the square, but what is being sold depends on the day of your visit. Some days it holds a fruit and vegetable market, but on others it's the usual tourist souvenirs.

Regardless of which day you visit, it's a busy square full of restaurants and cafes, and you will probably visit it more than once during your stay.

*Map 2.1 - The Square is looked over by a tall clock tower on the right-hand side. It is called the Torre dei Lamberti, so orientate yourself by facing the front of the tower.*

*Map 2.2 - Turn left to walk along the square to reach the Fontana Madonna Verona.*

## Fontana Madonna Verona

The tourists like to toss a coin into this pretty fountain, but if the market is in full swing you will have to navigate through the stalls to get to it.

It was commissioned by Cansignorio della Scala, who was Verona's last great leader before the city was taken over by the

Duke of Milan. Cansignorio had the fountain built to celebrate the arrival of clean water into Verona by a newly constructed aqueduct. The marble used to build the fountain was pinched from the ruins of the Roman Forum which lay here, and the fountain basin was taken from the old Roman Baths.

The basin is decorated with the faces of Verona's kings of long ago. The statue in the middle is called the Madonna Verona but has nothing to do with the Virgin Mary; she simply represents the beautiful city of Verona. The body of the Madonna is a recycled Roman statue which had lost both the head and the arms. So when it was decided to adorn the new fountain with it, a medieval head and arms were sculpted and added.

The Madonna Verona is holding a scroll which proclaims:

"Est iusti latrix urbs haec et laudis amatrix"
"This city is the bearer of justice and lover of public honour"

*Map 2.3 - Stand face to face with the Madonna and behind her you will see the beautiful Palazzo Maffei. Walk towards it.*

## Palazzo Maffei

The palazzo has stood here since the Middle Ages. It was built on top of part of the Campidoglio, the huge Roman temple which was dedicated to Jupiter, Juno, and Minerva.

The Palazzo was only two stories high when it was constructed and it was ornately decorated with columns and faces. In the seventeenth century the wealthy Marcantonio Maffei added the upper floor, and made sure it was equally ornate with eagles, inscriptions, and topped with a glorious balcony decorated with Apollo, Venus, Minerva, Mercury, Hercules, and Jupiter gazing down at you. Hercules, who stands on the left with hand on hip, is another recycled Roman statue, but his companions were all sculpted out of local marble.

Originally the roof held a garden which was famous across Europe. However gardens need water which resulted in the inside of the building being damaged by the moisture leeching down, so it was abandoned.

*In front of the palace is a lion-topped column.*

## St Marks Column

The lion is the symbol of Saint Mark, and Saint Mark is the patron saint of Venice. So every city which was ruled by Venice displayed the Lion of Venice.

The lion has a book between its front legs which represents wisdom and peace. However it didn't have a very peaceful existence as the lion was removed and destroyed by Napoleon's troops, and it took until 1886 to replace it.

*Face the Palazzo Maffei once more and look to its left-hand side to see the Torre del Gardello*

## Torre del Gardello

This tower replaced an even older tower. The replacement was commissioned by Cansignorio Della Scala in the thirteenth century, and it was built to be the tallest building in the city and visible from every part of Verona. The clock was one of the oldest in Europe although it stopped working in the seventeenth century. The locals still call the tower "the Tower of the Hours".

The bell from the tower was cast by Jacobus, one of the greatest bell makers of the time. It is now in the Castelvecchio museum. If you visit the museum on Walk 4 you can see the images Jacobus etched onto the bell, the Scaliger coat of arms and San Zeno who is the patron saint of Verona.

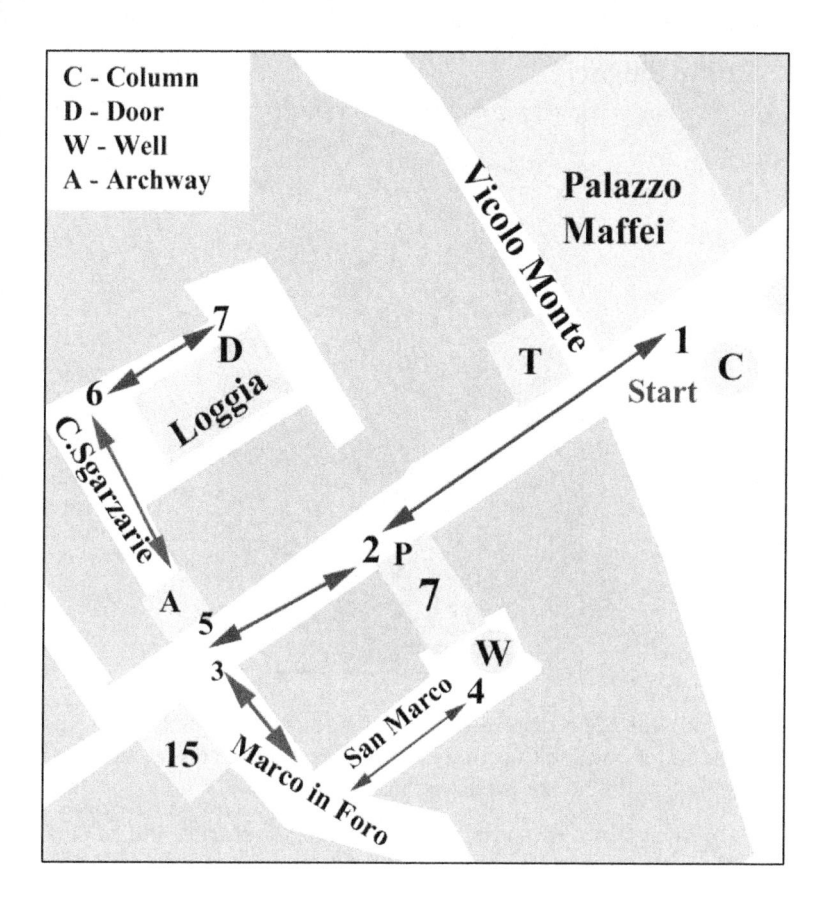

Map 3

*Map 3.1 - Face Palazzo Maffei and turn left into Corso Porta Borsai. Walk along to number 7 on your left.*

# Emilio Salgari

You will see a plaque with an image of Emilio Salgari on the wall, and if you look up there is another plaque commemorating his birth in the house you are standing outside.

He was a prolific writer of swashbuckler stories and science fiction. It's said that in Italy his works are more widely read than the much more famous Dante, and his stories are still translated for publication outside Italy. His tales have also been turned into cartoons and movies, and it's believed that Sergio Leone was inspired by Salgari's characters when creating the Spaghetti Western movies.

However despite his success he didn't earn much money. His beloved wife fell ill and he struggled to pay her medical bills. He killed himself and left a letter to the publishers of his stories:

> To you that have grown rich from the sweat of my brow while keeping myself and my family in misery, I ask only that from those profits you find the funds to pay for my funeral. I salute you while I break my pen.

*Map 3.2 - We move from one sad story to another. Continue along Corso Porta Borsai.*

*Map 3.3 - Turn left into Vicolo San Marco in Foro which is just before number 15. Just 10 meters on the left you will find a narrow alley called Pozzo San Marco. Go up it to find a pretty old well.*

## Corrado and Isabella

Corrado was a soldier who loved Isabella, but she did not return his passion. They met in the depths of winter beside this well, and Corrado in frustration accused her of being as cold as the ice in the well. She retorted by telling him to jump in the well to see how cold it was. He did and didn't resurface. Isabella suddenly realised how much she loved him and jumped in after him, and also drowned.

It used to be popular to throw a coin into the well for luck, but Verona has put a stop to that by sealing it.

*Map 3.4 - Backtrack down Pozzo San Marco, then right into Vicolo San Marco in Foro to rejoin Corso Porta Borsai.*

*You will see an old archway on the other side of Corso Porta Borsai*

## Corte Sgarzarie

Above the archway is a plaque which translates as:

> Here were the wool mills where the Common Veronese had so much luster and power from the third century to the fourteenth of the Common Era

For centuries wool was Verona's most important business and this area was where it was traded.

*Map 2.5 - Go under the archway into Corte Sgarzarie.*

You will see the old Loggia where business took place. It has been restored and is now a restaurant.

*Map 2.6 – Face the loggia and walk down the left hand to reach a green door.*

## Underground Verona

Behind that door is a stairway which leads down to the cryptoporticus, the underground complex of the Roman temple which once stood in this square.

The cryptoporticus was used as the city archive and was full of tablets and inscribed slabs. It was abandoned in the fourth century, and eventually collapsed due to neglect and flooding. It wasn't until the fourteenth century that historians started to investigate and dig.

You can visit if you have pre-booked a time-slot.

*Map 2.7 - Return along Corte Sgarzarie and go back through the archway.*

*Turn left along Corso Porta Borsai to return to the front of the Palazzo Mafei.*

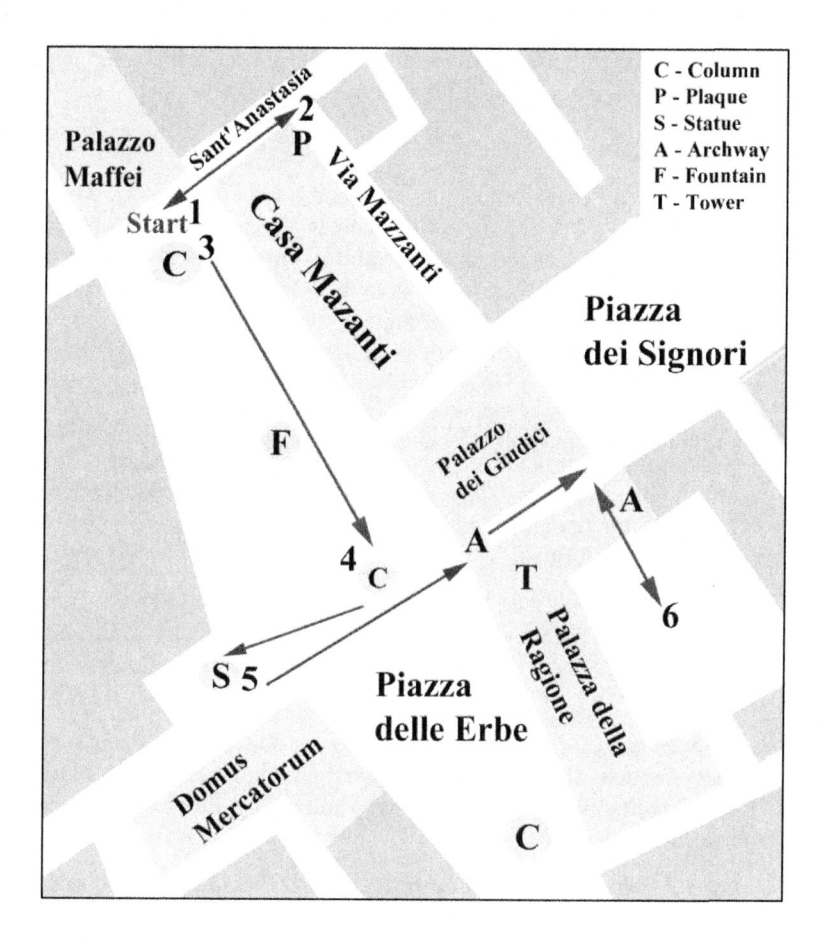

Map 3

***Map 3.1 - Walk between the Palazzo and the lion column, and walk straight ahead to take a few steps into Corso Sant'Anastasia. You will reach Via Mazzanti on your right***

## Via Mazzanti

This street is named after the last owner of Casa Mazzanti which is the building on your right - you will see the best façade of the Casa in a few minutes.

45

On your right you can see a steep iron stairway which leads up to the first floor and beneath it a plaque.

**Pasque Veronese**

The plaque commemorates a massacre which occurred when the citizens of Verona revolted against the army of Napoleon Bonaparte. It happened at Easter and is known as the Veronese Easter, or Pasque Veronese - as it says on the plaque. Any French person in Verona was murdered regardless of age or sex – in fact they even killed some unlucky Veronese who were thought to be French.

The massacre started on April 17 and finished on April 25 when the French army marched in to restore order. The consequences were a disaster for Verona. The main ringleaders were shot by firing squad and all other leaders were sent to prison in French Guyana.

Napoleon also made Verona pay a huge amount in reparation, and took the chance to confiscate many works of art and ship them to Paris – Napoleon did that all over Europe whenever he got the chance.

Napoleon then used the massacre as the perfect excuse to invade Venice. On May 12 1787, the thousand year old Venetian Republic was dissolved. Verona was later handed over to Austria as part of a treaty.

*Map 3.2 - Now backtrack and turn left into Piazza delle Erbe once more.*

*Stand with the Palazzo Maffei behind you. On your left is the pretty facade of the Casa Mazzanti.*

# Casa Mazzanti

This wonderful building will probably already have caught your eye as you walked through the square.

In the thirteenth century the top floor was used as a granary and the lower floor was a market hall.

In the fifteenth century it became very common in Italy to show off your wealth by either building a tall tower, or decorating your home with colourful frescoes. This one has a balcony running along the second floor and behind it a colourful fresco by Cavalli with allegories of Ignorance, Greed, Love, and Moderation. The frescoes are in pretty good condition considering they have been there for about five hundred years.

Verona used to have hundreds of buildings decorated like this, but sadly most are gone. As far back as 500 AD, Verona was named "urbs picta" in Latin, "The painted city" because of the frescoes.

*Map 3.3 - With Casa Mazzanti on your left, walk past the Madonna fountain to approach the high Torre dei Lamberti once more.*

*Just before you reach it you will see a four-columned marble canopy which is called the Capitello*

## Capitello

It's from the 13th century and this was where the city's governors sat to take their vows of office.

You will see carved into the stone two medieval units of measurement, the Tile and the Brick. They were used to check market goods to ensure traders weren't cheating their customers. If the goods being sold didn't meet the standard measurements the trader was punished – presumably making use of the manacle which you can see hanging down from the bottom step on one side

*Below the Torre dei Lamberti you will see an archway which is called the Arco della Costa.*

## Arco della Costa

The name means The Arch of the Coast which is a bit odd since Verona lies over 100 kilometers from the sea. However you will notice that a whale rib bone is suspended by an iron chain from the archway and some think that is the reason for the strange name.

It's a bit of a mystery as to why the rib bone is there but there are various theories. One of the best is that it's just an advert. Piazza delle Erbe was a busy marketplace and it's thought that an apothecary hung the bone on the arch to catch the eye of passing potential customers. It might be just a coincidence that the actual owner of the rib is the pharmacy which sits under the archway!

Local legend tells us that the rib bone will fall onto the first truthful person to walk under the archway. The archway gives access to the Piazza dei Signori which is full of buildings once used by Verona's lawyers and rulers, so those lawyers and politicos would certainly have walked under the archway many times. Even Popes have walked under it and the rib bone hasn't fallen yet - perhaps the legend is an ironic joke.

Above the archway a corridor runs between the Town Hall on the right and the Court on the left. Lawyers and politicians used the arch to cross between the two important establishments, without having to mingle with the common people below.

*Map 3.4 - Stand with the Arco della Costa behind you and the Capitello on your right. Cross the road In front of you to reach a very small Piazzetta which is home to a statue called Justice.*

## Justice

Justice stands with a sword dramatically raised to the sky.

It commemorates the bombing of this area by Austrian planes in 1915 during World War I - 29 people were killed and many more were injured. The statue was placed here in 1920, five years after the bombing. It's by a sculptor from Verona, Egidio Gireli, and this was his first attempt at a statue in bronze.

*Just next to Justice stands the Domus Mercatorum.*

## Domus Mercatorum

This was where the tradesmen and guildsmen of Verona met to make deals, barter, and generally run business in Verona.

The first building was just wooden but a member of the Scaliger family, Alberto, had it rebuilt in stone and in style, complete with a statue of the Madonna at one corner.

*Now turn your attention to the Torre dei Lamberti once more. The tower sits above the Palazza della Ragione*

## Palazza delle Ragione

It was after the twelfth century earthquake that Verona decided to build a town hall on this spot. It was originally called the Palazzo del Comune.

It burned in a fire in 1218, but Verona rebuilt it just one year later. It originally had four towers but only two have survived to today, the elegant Torre dei Lamberti and the stumpy tower which stands to the right. The Town Hall was renamed as the Palazzo delle Ragione in the fifteenth century when Verona was under Venetian rule.

## Torre dei Lamberti

The tower was built in the twelfth century by the Lamberti family and that tower was significantly lower than the one you see now. You can see the where the old tower ends and the new one begins by the marked difference in building materials about halfway up.

The Torre dei Lamberti was hit by lightning and badly damaged at the start of the fifteenth century. It took sixty years before it was restored, but Verona built it much taller and added the lovely octagonal bell tower at the same time, so it was worth the wait.

The Torre dei Lamberti got its clock in the eighteenth century. The clock on the older Torre del Gardello which you saw at the other end of Piazza delle Erbe had not worked for some time, so wealthy Count Giovanni Sagramoso paid for a clock to be added out of his own pocket.

*Map 3.5 - Now go through the Arco della Costa – it's unlikely the whale bone will fall on you!*

*Once through the arch you will find an archway on your right which takes you into the courtyard of the Town Hall.*

## Going up the tower

Near the entrance you will find the door to the ticket office for the tower. It's worth going up for the view. If you have a Verona card, entrance is included. You can either climb the 368 steps or take the lift. Irritatingly even if you have a Verona Card, you will be asked for another Euro for the privilege of using the elevator!

Once you get up there, try to spot the places you have already visited or plan to visit. You can even see the top of the old city wall climbing the distant hills.

**The Bells**

The octagonal bell chamber is home to four bells, three on the level you have access to and one more on the floor above.

Marangona is the middle of the three which you can see, and it was used to signal fire as well as to mark the hours of the day.

Later two smaller bells called The Bell of the Hours and Rabbiosa were placed on either side of it. The smaller bells are now used to mark the hours.

The biggest bell, Rengo, is one floor up and out of sight – it was a call to arms. It was Rengo that rang out at the end of World War I in 1918.

*Descend and return to the Palazza delle Ragione courtyard.*

Northern Italy suffered a terrible famine in the sixteenth century and this courtyard was used to sell flour to the poor at affordable prices. Take a few minutes to admire the wonderful staircase which is called the Stairs of Reason.

*Climb the red marble stairs to reach the entrance to the Museum of Modern Art which is included in your tower ticket. If you don't want to visit, continue this walk from "Exiting the Museum" on page 55.*

## Galleria d'Arte Moderna Achille Forti

The museum was founded by Archille Forti, who left his estate and his modern art collection to fund and kick-start the new museum.

If you visit, be prepared to spend more time than you might expect as it's full of interesting works. Even if you are not a modern art fan, it's worth visiting to see the wonderful ancient and vaulted Cappella dei Notai which is full of much earlier religious paintings.

Here are some highlights to look for as you explore:

**Francesco Hayez - Meditazione**

The lady represents Italy of two hundred years ago, when it was still not one country and large parts were ruled by France and Austria. The cross held by the young woman is inscribed with the dates of the Five Days of Milan, a battle in the first war of Italian Independence.

The sad eyes of Italy mourn the restoration of Austrian rule in the Veneto region. The eyes are meant to remind the viewer of the lives lost in the battle to oust foreign rule.

## Angelo Dall'Oca - Foglie cadenti

Angelo Dall'Oca Bianca was born in Verona. He exhibited at many international exhibitions and he was awarded a gold medal for this painting in Barcelona in 1896.

It shows a church in the background and many people walking past. Your eye is drawn to the modest young woman at the front as she passes the men with downcast eyes.

## Ettore Beraldini - I vecchi

Here we see a gathering of elderly gentlemen, with one curious old chap on the right looking out at you the viewer.

**Pino Casarini - Figure sul lago**

It's just so eye-catching, so a personal favourite.

*Find your way to the Chapel of the Notaries – you might have to ask for directions from the staff.*

### Cappella dei Notai – The Chapel of the Notaries

This chapel was added when the lawyers exited and moved into the Palazzo delle Ragione.

This low arched chamber with its intricately painted decoration and golden framings is really beautiful,

Sadly what you see now are not the original paintings, as they were lost in a fire. The replacements were added in the eighteenth century but they are still very beautiful.

The chapel is popular as a wedding venue which must be a colourful event.

## Exiting the Museum

*Map 3.6 - When you exit the museum, go down the stairs and turn left to exit the courtyard.*

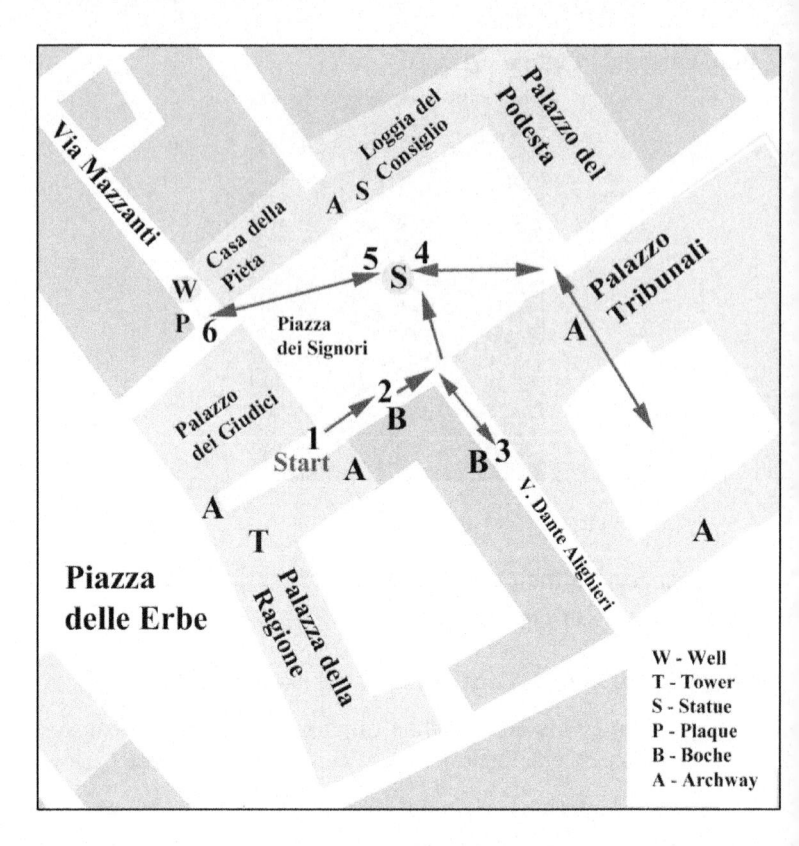

Map 4

***Map 4.1 - Turn right to enter Piazza dei Signori.***

As you do, find the little post-box on the wall of the building on your right-hand side. It's called a Boche de Leon meaning a Lion's Mouth, and they were installed in cities ruled by Venice.

## Boche de Leon for Moneylending

> E CONTRATI
> USURATICI DI
> QUALUNQUE SORTE

The Lion's Mouth post-boxes were for the use of anyone who wanted to report a crime to the council. However you had to be very sure of your accusation, as the magistrate who read your report would burn it if you and a witness hadn't signed it.

There were many such post-boxes in the cities ruled by Venice, and each one stated which crimes it was interested in. This one was for reporting usury, or money lending as we know it, which was strictly forbidden to Christians.

*Map 4.2 - Just past the postbox is Via Dante Alighieri. Go down it to find a second post-box on your right.*

## Boche de Leon for Silk Smuggling

This post-box was for reporting anyone who smuggled silk or illegally cultivated mulberry bushes on which silkworms lived.

In the sixteenth century huge swathes of the lands around Verona were used to grow mulberry bushes to produce raw silk. Silk was highly taxed and earned a huge amount of money for Verona – so the government came down heavily on anyone trying to evade paying tax on it - if you were caught you were likely to be executed!

*Map 4.3 - Return to Piazza dei Signori. Approach the statue in the middle.*

## Piazza dei Signori

This is usually a very busy square. It was the centre of power in Verona, so all around it are the most important buildings which were used to run the city and the courts.

## Dante

Centre stage stands a Carrara marble statue of a thoughtful looking Dante.

It was added in 1865 to celebrate the sixth centenary of his birth. He is Italy's most famous poet and hailed from Florence.

He was a Guelph, a political group which supported the Pope as opposed to the Ghibellines who supported the Monarchy. The Guelphs and the Ghibellines argued and fought with each other all over Italy. After one particular victory in 1302 the Guelphs were exiled from Florence, and if Dante had returned to his home city he would have been burned at the stake. That sentence was only rescinded by Florence in 2008!

Dante fled Florence and wandered around Italy. He lived in Verona from 1312 until 1318 and was made welcome by Cangrande I. It was while in Verona that he wrote a large part of his most famous poem, "The Divine Comedy". He worked at his masterpiece in the Capitular Library near the Cathedral – you will see it on Walk 3. The poem describes in detail the horrors and tortures awaiting sinners in hell. Dante liked to retaliate against his accusers in Florence by dropping them into the various circles of hell in his epic tale.

He is now so revered in Italy that they put his image on one of their coins, a bit like Shakespeare on the British twenty pound note. Also Asteroid 2999 Dante was named after him. The locals call this square Piazza Dante.

*Stand face to face with Dante and you will see a yellow building behind him to the right – it has an arcade on the ground floor.*

# Loggia del Consiglio

This is thought to be one of Verona's most beautiful buildings and is from the fifteenth century. It was built to host the city council and no expense was spared in its construction.

## Fra Giocondo

Take a moment to look at the lovely stone work which runs up the columns of the 8 arches and all around the upper floor windows.

Look above the left-hand column and you will see a sculpted figure pointing into a book. That is Fra Giocondo who designed the Loggia. He came from Verona and became a monk, but was also a renowned architect who designed or worked on beautiful buildings all over Italy – including Florence Cathedral.

**Pliny the Elder**

Right at the top stands a group of statues, who are all well-known citizens of Verona from the past.

The most famous is probably the middle statue which is Pliny the Elder - a Roman military commander, philosopher, naturalist, and writer. He died in AD 79 trying to rescue friends from the eruption of Mount Vesuvius which had already buried Pompeii and Herculaneum under ash. His ship could not escape the Harbour and was sunk during a subsequent eruption. It should be mentioned that no-one is actually certain where Pliny came from, and the other city claiming him as a son is Como in northern Italy.

*To the left of the Loggia you will see the Arco della Tortura.*

## Arco della Tortura

It's said that long ago the instruments of torture used to get the required answers from criminals were suspended from the archway. It's ironic that the statue above the arch is Girolamo Fracastoro who was a doctor.

# Girolamo Fracastoro and Syphilis

He was much loved by the people of Verona because he would treat the poor for free. He is famous for a poem which is 1,300 verses long and called:

Syphilis Sive de Morbo Gallico
Syphilis or the French Disease

The poem tells us that the shepherd Sifilo was the first victim of the disease – inflicted on him by Apollo because Sifilo stopped worshipping him. Sifilo was cured by Juno, the wife of Jupiter. She told him to apply leaves from the guaiacum tree, and a friendly nymph hinted that mercury would also help – both real cures. It was a clever ruse by the doctor to spread the knowledge of the disease and how to cure it by writing the poem. It was translated into many languages and was widely read,

He also came up with the idea that infections are caused by little germ bodies from infected items which are spread by touch or by air.

Girolamo is holding a ball which symbolises the Earth, and here we have another of Verona's legends. It's said the ball will fall onto the first honourable person to walk under the arch. However just like the whale's rib, it's still in place.

*On the left side of the arch stands the Casa della Pieta.*

# Casa della Pièta

This is the House of Charity. You will see a sculpture of a seated woman holding a flag on the first floor. It was placed there when Verona fell under Venetian rule, and represents Verona safe under Venetian protection.

The building also houses the oldest coffee shop in Verona if you feel the need. It has always been a favourite of Verona's artists, writers, and politicians who came to discuss and debate everything which was wrong in the world.

*Stand face to face with Dante again and this time turn right. The building in front of you is the Palazzo del Podesta.*

# Palazzo del Podestà

This was the base of the Scaliger family and they liked to welcome artists. Giotto was a famous visitor, as was Dante. He stayed here during his long exile and in gratitude he added a verse to "The Divine Comedy" celebrating the Scaliger family:

> Your first refuge, the first hostel
> it will be the courtesy of the great Lombard
> that on the ladder carries the holy bird.

The Scaliger family originated in Lombardy, hence "the great Lombard" in Dante's verse. Also the name Scaliger comes from Scala meaning Ladder, an emblem which the family used in their coat of arms. The holy bird is the eagle which was used by the Scaligers in their role as vicars of "The Holy Roman Empire".

When Dante's statue was designed, the poet was cast inclining his head towards this palace in gratitude to the Scaliger family for giving him refuge.

The building's most striking feature is its ornate doorway. When Venice took over, this palace continued to house the governor of the city. Which probably explains why the Lion stands above the doorway – the lion was the symbol of Venice. Beneath the lion you can read the name of the Venetian Doge who commissioned the door, Giovanni Dolfin.

The inner courtyard was once covered in ornate frescoes added by Giotto during his stay, but they have not survived.

*Now stand facing the same way as Dante, and take a look at the building to the left of the archway.*

## Palazzo Tribunali or Palazzo di Cansignorio

This was built in the sixteenth century for Cansignorio della Scala. It was originally a fortress guarded by three towers – only one stands now. It is where Verona's court has been housed since the start of the nineteenth century.

*Map 3.4 - The Palazzo has an archway which gives you access to the large inner courtyard. Go through the archway to enter the courtyard which the locals call "The Court of the Court".*

# The Courtyard

Once in the courtyard you will see the Porta dei Bombardieri opposite you, it is decorated with cannons, torches, gunpowder barrels and other pieces of lethal weaponry. It was commissioned by Verona's artillery company who had their headquarters in this palazzo.

In the middle of the courtyard you can peer into two glassed over excavation areas to see Roman ruins and part of a floor decorated with a mosaic.

***Return to the Piazza and stand face to face with Dante once more.***
***Turn left and the building in front of you is the Palazzo dei Giudici.***

# Palazzo dei Giudici

This imposing building was where Verona's judges lived and at the time of writing is a hotel.

*Map 3.5 - Before leaving this lovely square, stand face to face with Dante and cross the square diagonally left.*

*You will find an archway which will take you into Via Mazzanti which you visited earlier.*

# Pozzo Mazzanti

Here you will find a lovely old well made of red marble with two columns. The residents in the nearby buildings were able to lower buckets from their windows into the well saving a bit of a chore climbing down and back up again.

Unfortunately the well now has a nasty crack along it, so let's hope Verona gets it restored soon.

A plaque on the wall near the well commemorates where Mastino Della Scala was assassinated. It sits just below the first floor window of number 1a.

Mastino was the first of the Scaligers to hold real power but he still came to a messy end. No-one knows for sure who killed him but it's thought to have been one of Verona's other powerful families.

***Map 3.6 – Back-track to the Piazza dei Signori and stand facing the same way as Dante one last time.***

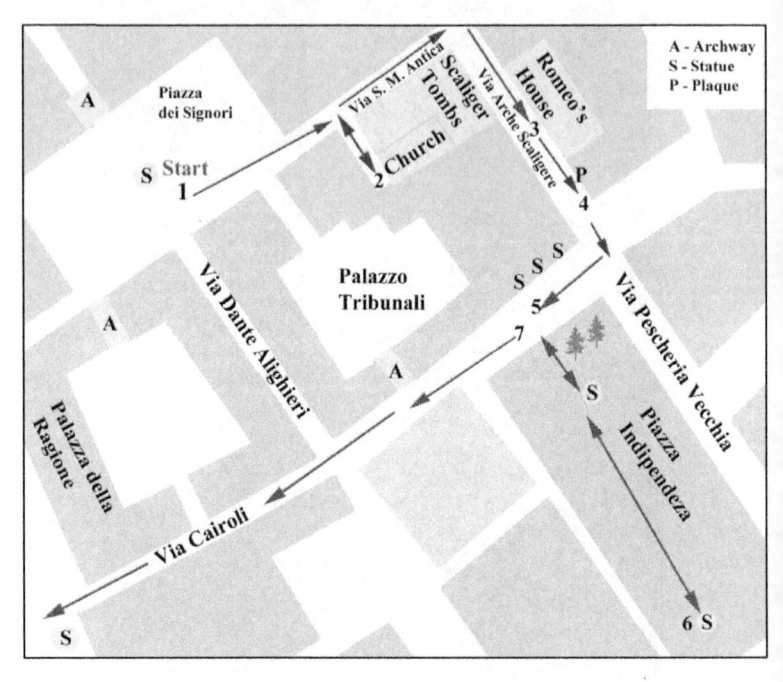

Map 4

***Map 4.1 - Turn diagonally left to go under another archway and leave the square by Via Santa Maria Antica. You will immediately find the Scaliger Tombs on your right.***

## Scaliger Tombs

This group of Gothic tombs holds the remains of the Scaliger family who ruled Verona for so long. The tombs sit behind an iron fence but you can purchase a ticket to get a closer look – or use your Verona Card.

As you explore the tomb area you will see many ladders sculpted into the stonework and the iron railings, because the ladder is part of the Scaliger coat of arms – remember Scala means steps.

**Cangrande I**

Cangrande I lies in a marble tomb above the church door. At the top we see him on his horse smiling and wearing a helmet in the shape of dog's head, very fitting for Big Dog 1. Below the statue lies his sarcophagus, guarded by two dogs holding the

Scala coat of arms. On the side of the sarcophagus is a list of his military victories and the armies he defeated

He was the most successful and famous of the Scaligers. He expanded the territory ruled by the Scaliger family, but was also a great patron of the arts. When he died his family organised a very ornate funeral to send him on his way. The equestrian statue is not the original of course – it is safely stashed in the Castelvecchio museum, so you might see it if you tackle Walk 4.

Verona is very fond of this statue. It appears on various logos, including that of Chievo – one of Verona's football teams. It is also on the labels of some Valpolicella wine bottles.

You will see two pyramidal tombs in the railed-off area. Both have equestrian statues at the top, the one wearing a helmet with wings on it is Mastino II. The other one is Cansignorio.

**Cansignorio**

Cansignorio was a popular leader who reduced taxes, and when times were bad made sure there was cheap food for the poor. He also spent a lot of money making Verona a beautiful place with palaces and bridges.

**Mastino II**

Mastino II's tomb has four angels standing at the corners, and there are more angles on either side of the sarcophagus which is topped with a statue of Mastino.

The other smaller tombs hold the remains of the less important family members.

## Santa Maria Antica

The church behind the tombs was the private church of the Scala family, and the tombs you have just had a look at lie in the private cemetery of the church.

Verona has an interesting tradition on the 22nd May. As the sun rises, the local ladies come into the church to pray to the Saint of Impossible Causes, Santa Rita. There is a chapel dedicated to her.

She is believed to help abused wives and heartbroken women. The ladies leave roses at her altar, because as Rita lay dying she asked for a rose from her garden. It was winter but when her cousin next went into the garden he found a rose in flower. When Rita died all the bells in the village started to ring. She was declared a saint in 1900.

*Map 4.2 - From the church door, walk straight ahead, with the tombs on your right.*

*Turn right to walk along Via Santa Maria Antica, keeping the tombs on your right.*

*When you reach the first crossroads, turn right into Via Arche Scaligere. You will find Romeo's house at number 4 on your left.*

## Romeo's House

Did Romeo and Juliet exist? There is a similarity between the family names in Shakespeare's play, the Capulets and the Montagues, and two real rival families, the Montecci and the Cappelletti, who did indeed live in Verona.

The Montecci were exiled from Verona by Big Dog I when they were caught plotting against the Scaliger family. They were written about by Dante in his famous poem The Divine Comedy.

This house is called the Casa Montecci. It's known that the Montecci did live somewhere nearby but this house belonged to a quite different family. The house is really a small castle – often needed because assassination and feuds were common in Italy at the time, mostly between the Guelphs and the Ghibelline factions. The fact that it is called Romeo's House is really to please the tourists. It's a private house so you can't visit.

There is an inscription on the facade of the house that reads:

*O where is Romeo*
*Tut, I have lost myself, I am not here:*
*This is not Romeo, he's some other where.*

Perhaps the owners of the house are trying to tell us something?

*Map 4.3 - Walk past the house to the restaurant next door at number 2.*

# Romeo's exile

There is a little plaque on the facade which shows us Romeo on his horse going into exile. It was while he was in exile that he heard about Juliet's death.

*Map 4.4 - Continue along Via Arche Scaligere and take the first right into Piazza Indipendenza.*

# Gingko Trees

Standing at the corner of Via Arche Scaligere and Piazza Independenza are two Gingko trees. If you are lucky to be here in autumn you will see that the foliage has turned a glorious yellow. The locals make special trips to this square to see the golden cloud.

*The building on your right-hand side is the back of the Palazzo Tribunali which you visited earlier.*

# Palazzo Tribunali Again

On the facade are busts of three renowned politicians who are seen as Italian heroes, Benedetto Cairoli, Cesare Battisti, and Giacomo Matteotti.

Cairoli and Battisti were both fervent campaigners and fighters for Italian Unification. Giacomo Matteotti campaigned against Mussolini and was executed by the Fascists.

*Map 4.5 - Now cross the road and walk into the square to find Verona's statue of Garibaldi.*

## Giuseppe Garibaldi

You read about Garibaldi in the potted history. He was the military leader who battled for Italian Independence and united Southern Italy, so it's fitting that his statue stands here in Independence Square.

*Behind Garibaldi is a little square where you can take a breather in a welcome spot of greenery.*

It also sports a statue of Romeo and Juliet, although you might not recognize them!

## Romeo e Giulietta, un sogno sospeso

The bronze statue's title means Romeo and Juliet, a Suspended Dream.

It's a Polish piece of art which arrived in the square in 2012. It was part of a festival of European Stories, celebrating the 20th anniversary of the fall the Berlin Wall.

The two ill-fated lovers are shown as two hearts; it sits about halfway between "Juliet's House" and "Romeo's House".

The statue was created by Enrico Muscetra, an artist famous for his "hearts" sculptures.

*Map 4.6 - When you are ready to move on, return to the statue of Garibaldi.*

*Retrace your steps to the three politicians on the Palazzo Tribunali wall. Face them and turn left.*

*Map 4.7 – You will first pass three small arches on your right and then another archway which has a plaque at its side. That is the exit of the Porta dei Bombardieri which you saw earlier.*

*Map 4.8 - Continue walking along the side of the Palazzo Tribunali and you will walk straight into Via Cairoli. At its end turn you will find the statue of Berto Barbarani on your left.*

You have now reached the end of this walk.

# Walk 3 – The Churches and Bridges

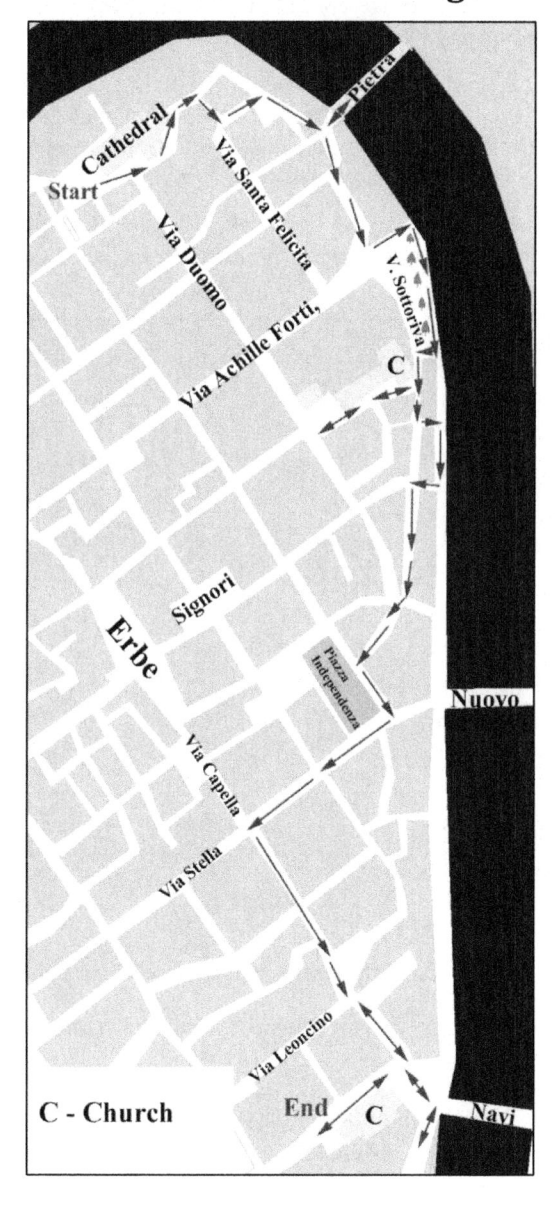

Overview Walk 3

This walk takes you to Verona's four major churches – which is useful if you have purchased the Churches Card which has to be used up in one day.

Three of the churches are within walking distance of each other, but the fourth is quite a way out. So make sure you have a copy of the Verona bus map and timetable before you set out. You can pick one up at the tourist office on Piazza Bra.

Remember to pick up an information leaflet as you enter each church. They are packed with information on what you can see inside.

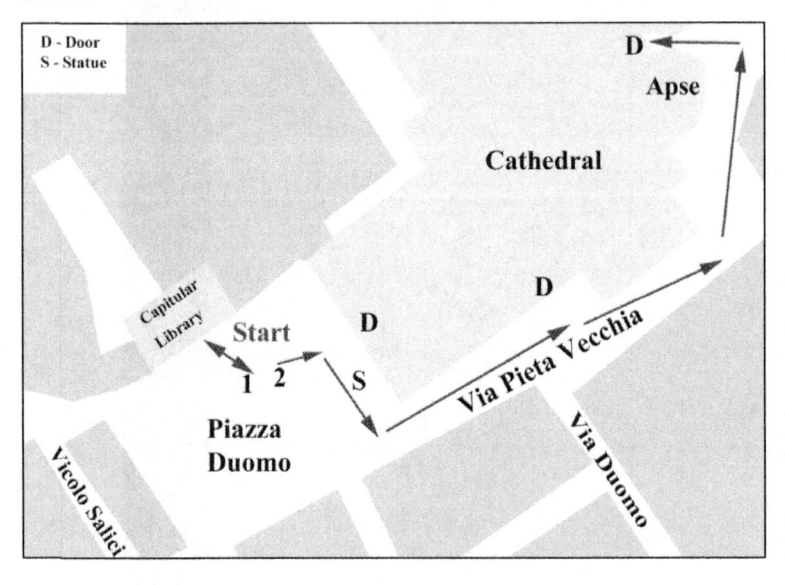

Map 1

*The walk starts at the Cathedral which sits on Piazza Duomo.*

*Map 1.1 - Stand in Piazza Duomo facing the main door of the cathedral and turn left.*

You will see a building with two chimneys. That is the Capitular Library of Verona, as it helpfully says on the door.

# Capitular Library of Verona

It is one of the treasures of Verona, and is said to be the oldest surviving library in the world.

It began in the fifth century AD as somewhere the priests could preserve their precious manuscripts and documents. The collection grew and grew as important papers and letters were deposited, and today its home to thousands of manuscripts, books, and even some ancient paintings.

In the fourteenth century letters from the Roman Consul Cicero to his friend Atticus were discovered here. Cicero's letters threw a shining light on the politics and struggles within Rome at that time. He believed passionately in the Roman Republic and argued in the Senate against both Julius Caesar and Mark Anthony, in an attempt to stop Rome falling under the control of the powerful military elite. Caesar was eventually assassinated, but Cicero was also later assassinated by Mark Anthony's troops.

Dante certainly visited the library and browsed around the books and documents during his long stay in Verona – even in his day the library was over 1000 years old.

Napoleon stole everything of value he could lay hands on when he took over Verona, and sent his loot to Paris. Only two thirds of the documents stolen from the library were returned by France.

If you love books, old libraries, and reading rooms, you will probably want to visit. You can buy a ticket, and tours are also available.

***When you are ready to continue, face the cathedral once more.***

# Verona Cathedral

The main door is guarded by two very weather-worn griffons and a striking angel in blue.

Walk up to the door which you will see is framed by layered arches. Spot the two warriors on either side of the outermost arch - they are Roland and Oliver.

**Roland and Oliver**

They are two of the twelve paladins of Charlemagne, the European equivalent of King Arthur's Knights of the Round Table. Their adventures are told in a poem from the eleventh century called "The Song of Roland" Roland wields an enchanted unbreakable sword called Durendal – a bit like Arthur's Excalibur.

Here Roland and Oliver guard the door to the Cathedral. Roland is on the left with his sword Durendal and Oliver is on the right bearing his mace. Behind them on the inner arches stand various saints from the Old Testament.

## Into the Cathedral

As with many cathedrals and important churches you can't use the front door. At the time of writing the entrance is at the back of the church.

*Map 1.2 - Walk down the right hand side of the cathedral on Via Pietà Vecchia. You will get a good view of the bell-tower as you do.*

*Walk to the end of the Cathedral and around the apse to find the tourist entrance.*

*Go inside. You will start in a little hall which lets you choose which of the three destinations to explore. Start with the Baptistery.*

**The Baptistery**

The highlight is the large font which was carved out of a single block of Verona marble. The font is octagonal as eight has a mystical meaning - it refers to the eighth day, Judgement Day, when everyone ends up in heaven or hell depending on how good they have been. If you look in the font you will see a second smaller font inside it which would take significantly less holy water to fill.

It's beautifully carved with key moments from the life of Jesus:

The Annunciation
The Visitation
The Nativity
The Three Kings
The Shepherds
Herod and his soldiers
The massacre of the innocents
The flight into Egypt

The Flight into Egypt has a lovely donkey carrying Mary – ready to take his next step on the journey with a raised hoof. In front of the donkey is Joseph - he is carrying Jesus in a pose more often associated with Saint Christopher, i.e. with Jesus on his shoulder.

Look closely at the little sculpture just next to Mary's left hand and you will see a cat with a rat in its mouth which is an oddity. Much more gruesome is The Massacre of the Innocents which shows us a disembowelled child.

On the walls are some frescoes from the thirteenth century. Look into the little chapel to the right of the altar to see a fresco of the Virgin Mary sheltering mankind with her cloak. The modern statue of an angel which stands on the left of the fresco is particularly beautiful.

*Return to the little hall and this time head for church of Santa Elena.*

*To reach it you will first pass through what was a passageway between the Cathedral and Santa Elena, and which is now being excavated.*

**Another Bone**

Pause just before the steps to the glass door which take you into Santa Elena. Look up to the left and you will see a bone hanging from the ceiling. This one has nothing to do with advertising like the one on Piazza delle Erbe. No-one really knows why it's here, but it's thought it probably represents the killing of a monstrous being such as a dragon by Christian crusaders.

*Now go into Santa Elena.*

## Santa Elena

The cathedral area is a very old site for religious buildings. It started with a Roman temple to the goddess Minerva. In the fourth century Saint Zeno built the first Christian church here, which was then replaced by a church dedicated to Saint Zeno himself in the ninth century. That church collapsed in the huge earthquake in the twelfth century. The church of Santa Elena was built to replace it soon after.

The excavated floor areas let you see down to the mosaic floor and foundations of the older churches.

When you are ready to move on, return to the hall. Now it's time to enter the Cathedral itself. You will enter on one side of the altar.

## The Cathedral

Your first impression will be "pink" as it's full of pink marble. Walk down the church to the main door. Face the door and turn right to find the chapel which contains a work by Titian.

**Titian**

This is a painting of the Assumption by Titian – real name Tiziano Vecellio. It has his trademark red being worn by some of the disciples as they watch the Virgin Mary rising up to heaven. The painting was pinched by Napoleon but returned once he was defeated.

Facing the painting, turn right to walk down the left hand side of the Cathedral. About half way down you will find a chapel much loved by the locals. It contains a beautiful golden Madonna and Child.

Now return to the centre of the church. Walk down between the wonderfully pink columns passing the altar to reach the circular chapel behind it. Look up to the dome. There you will see the disciples watching The Virgin Mary ascend to heaven, and as they do they are cleverly painted as though leaning on and over the balustrade. It's more eye-catching and lively than the Titian painting of the same scene which you just looked at.

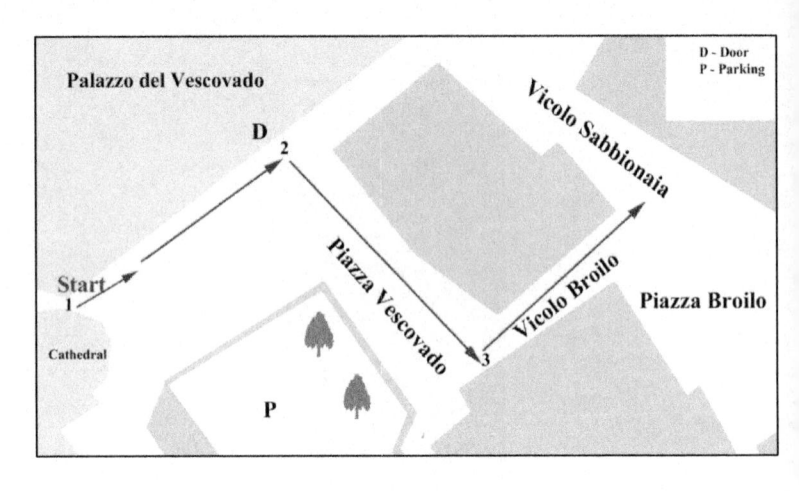

Map 2

*Map 2.1 - Exit the cathedral.*

*You will see what's left of a very elderly building on your right.*

At the time of writing it is being held up by braced beams and being used as a carpark.

## Palazzo del Vescovado

On your left-hand side is the Palazzo del Vescovado which is Bishop's Palace. Walk along the front to reach its ornate door which is topped with the Virgin Mary and some saints.

*Map 2.2 - Face away from the door and walk straight ahead into Piazza Vescovado.*

*Map 2.3 - When you reach the end of the piazza, turn left into Vicolo Broilo which is a very short street. At its end turn right into Piazza Broilo.*

A - Archway
M - Memorial
F - Frescoes

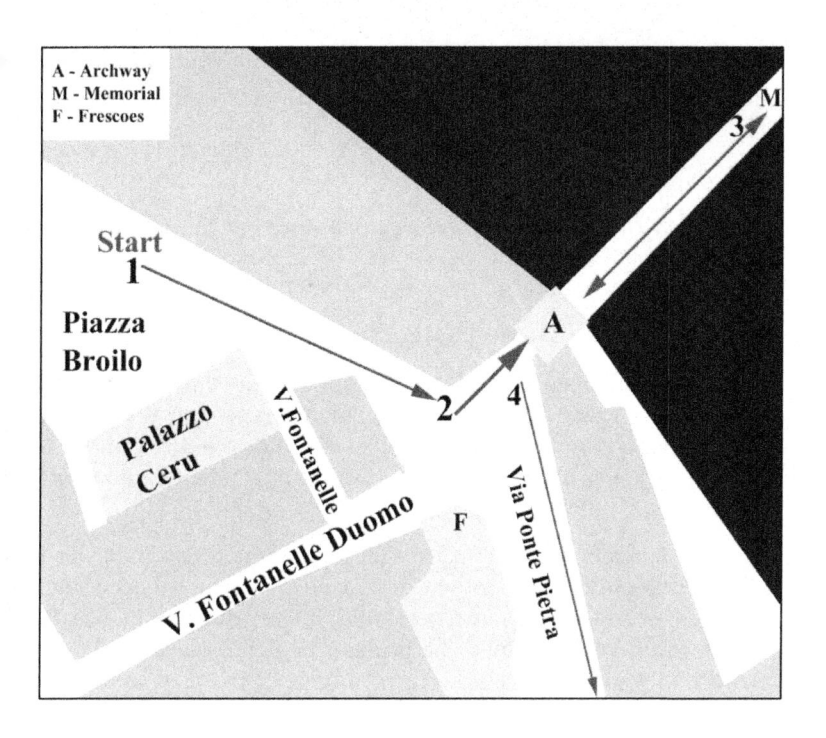

Map 3

## Piazza Briolo

The square's name comes from the Latin word broilum, which was a place where fruit and vegetables were grown. This was the Bishop's orchard and vegetable garden.

On your left-hand side you can see the Palazzo degli Asili with its four Corinthian columns in the first floor.

Palazzo Ceru runs across the bottom of the square. It has a lovely central balcony and windows which are held in pink marble. During World War II the local people sheltered in the Palazzo Ceru's deep cellars during air raids.

*Map 3.1 - Walk straight ahead to the other end of the square. Palazzo Ceru will be on your on your right.*

*Pass a little street called Vicoletto Fontanelle on your right, and a few more steps will take you to a crossroads.*

On your left you will find a tower and archway which gives access to the Stone Bridge.

*Map 3.2 - Go through the archway and walk out to the middle of the bridge.*

## Ponte Pietra (Stone Bridge)

There has been a river crossing at this spot for as long as Verona has existed. This is where the current is at its slowest because of the wide bend the river water has to get round. So a bridge here was likely to last longer than anywhere else along the Adige. Well that was the theory.

The Romans built the first stone bridge replacing the original wooden version. It was then destroyed by nature and by man over the centuries, but always rebuilt. Its last incarnation was in 1957 when Verona fished the bridge fragments out of the river where they landed when the retreating Germans blew up all the river bridges.

At one time there was a matching tower on the far side of the bridge but it was taken down in the nineteenth century. The furthest two bridge arches are the only survivors from Roman Times – they are built of white stone. The other arches have had to be rebuilt over the centuries and they are made of rather less interesting brick.

In the middle of the bridge you will see an old memorial stone. At one time it was covered by graffiti, but the Angels of Beauty have restored it and still guard it from any further vandalism.

In case you don't manage to fit Walk 5 in, look over to the right and you will see St Peters Castle looming over the city and surrounded by high pine trees. Beneath the castle is what's left of the Roman Theatre.

Now look left. You will see the domed Santuario della Madonna di Lourdes sitting on a hill some distance away.

If you are in Verona long enough and feel the need to get out of the city, you could catch a bus up to the sanctuary, enjoy the view of Verona as shown above, and then stroll down the hill and back over the river.

*Map 3.3 - When you are ready to continue with this walk, retrace your steps and go under the archway once more.*

Once through the archway, look to the top of the very old building on the other side of the road – it sits on the corner of Vicolo Fontanelle Duomo. You will see some surviving frescoes just underneath the roof. Again they really need some vital restoration work.

*Map 3.4 - Now turn left to walk along Via Ponte Pietra. You will see the tower of your next church destination, Santa Anastasia, in front of you.*

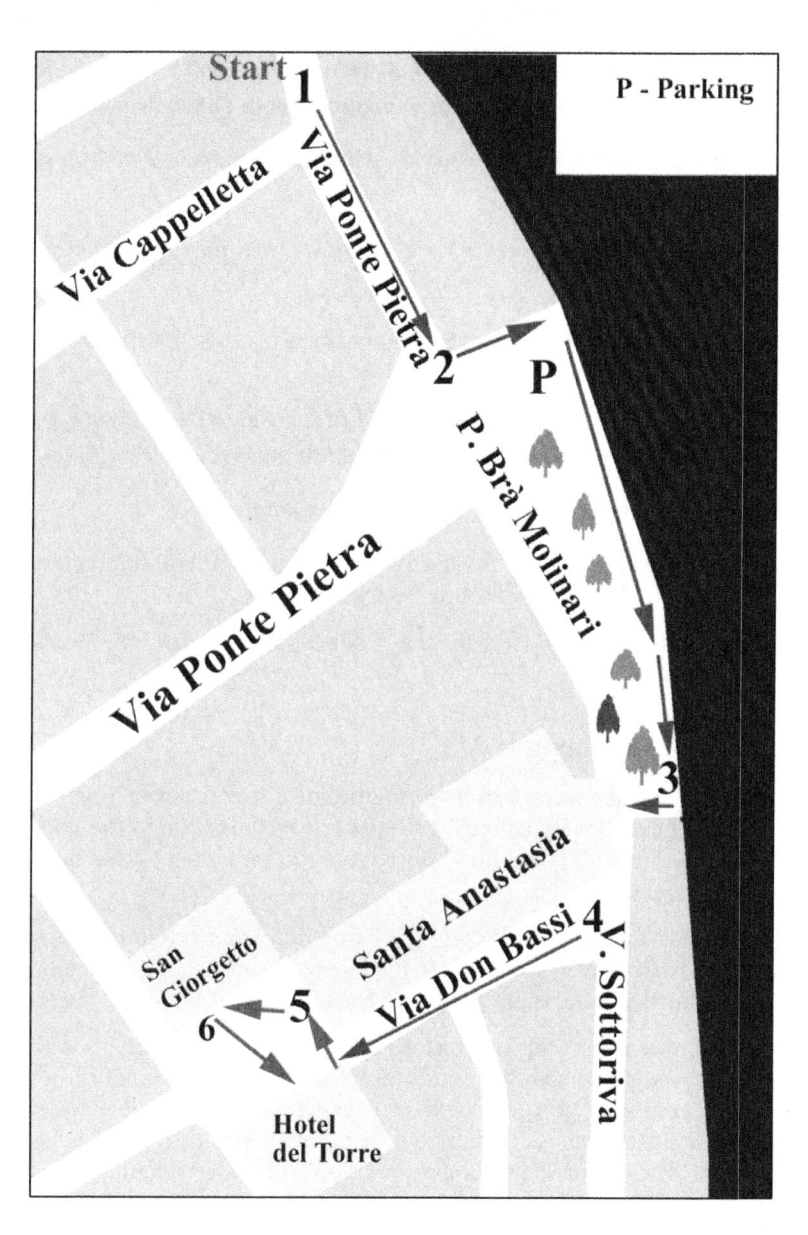

Map 4

*Map 4.1 - Pass Via Cappelletta on your right. Continue along Via Ponte Pietra – enjoy the lovely windows on your right as you do.*

*You will reach a wide crossroads which is a bit spoiled by a busy car-par on the left.*

*Map 4.2 - Turn left to reach the river-side then turn right to stroll along it.*

You can see the apse of Santa Anastasia on you right-hand side as you walk along the riverside.

*Map 4.3 – When you reach the end of the river-side pathway, go down the steps on the right and turn left into narrow Via Sottoriva.*

*Map 4.4 - Take the first right into Via Don Bassi.*

As you walk along the side of the church you will appreciate that Santa Anastasia is Verona's largest church.

*You will eventually reach the front of the church on Piazza Anastasia.*

## Santa Anastasia

The façade is very uninspiring because it was never finished. It does have lovely colourful stonework arching around the door – so we can only imagine how lovely the rest would have been had it been finished.

Look to the right of the right-hand door to see two cravings. They both concern Saint Peter the Martyr – a local Saint Peter and not the much more famous one in the bible.

This Saint Peter was renowned for his conversations with martyred saints and for other miracles. The bottom relief shows him preaching to the crowd in Verona. He was challenged by non-believers to ask God to give shade to his sweltering audience. Saint Peter prayed and God immediately provided a handy cloud to give relief to the faithful – you can see the cloud shielding Peter and his audience.

It was originally planned to put more sculptures on the other side of the door but that never happened.

Go inside to see a beautiful church, wonderfully colourful from the floor to the ceiling.

The floor is covered with red marble from Verona, interspersed with black and white stone, the red represents the blood of Christ, and the black and white represents the traditional colours of the Dominicans who owned the church. The vaulted ceiling is covered in swirling decoration, and the walls are full of frescoes – even the columns have frescoes on them.

**The Hunchbacks**

The twelve columns lead you towards the altar. Spot the two basins at the bottom of the first two columns which are held up by two little hunchbacked men. They represent the huge labour of the people of Verona in building this church.

The one on the left seems a very poor and sad little hunchback - it was sculpted by the eldest son of Veronese, Gabriele Caliari. The one on the right is bigger – it was sculpted by a different artist, Paolo Orefice. It's said to be lucky to touch the hunch of either of the hunchbacks.

## Mary Magdalene

Walk up the right hand side of the church. About halfway up you will reach a painting of Mary Magdalene accompanied by two other saints. What is interesting is the depiction of Mary Magdalene modestly hidden behind her hair which reaches her feet. The legend is that Mary took herself to the desert after the resurrection and basically prayed for the rest of her life. Her clothes became rags and fell off, so her hair grew rapidly to provide some cover.

Walk up to the main altar. Facing the altar turn to your left and then walk straight ahead into the Giusti chapel

## Giusti Chapel

If you go into the chapel you will see it has a beautiful old wooden choir in dark wood. Look up and you will see an odd-looking piece of wood suspended from the ceiling. It's an old ship rudder and is a trophy from the battle of Lepanto, a momentous naval battle which took place in Greece in 1571. It was one of the few occasions when the nations of Europe stood together rather than battling each other, and it was the deciding battle which halted the Ottoman invasion of Europe.

Now leave the chapel and cross the church to reach the other side. There are two chapels on the right-hand side of the altar. The one furthest from the altar is the Cavalli chapel.

**Cavalli Chapel**

Once you are inside the chapel, look up to your right near the entrance. That fresco was commissioned by the Cavalli family, and since they paid for it they are in it.

The Cavalli men are dressed in full armour and are kneeling in front of the Virgin Mary and Jesus. They are accompanied by Saint George, Saint Martin and Saint James. Below the fresco and attached to the wall lies the tomb of Frederico Cavalli in red Verona marble – he is the Cavalli nearest the Virgin Mary in the fresco.

Now visit the chapel just next door, the Pellegrini chapel. Look up above the entrance to see Pisanello's famous fresco – its high above you so you will have to stand well back to see it.

## Pisanello's fresco

It shows us the legend of St George and the Dragon. Originally the fresco was much larger but only two parts have survived and only one is in good condition. We see a blond curly-haired St George about to get on his horse. The dragon lies defeated behind St George.

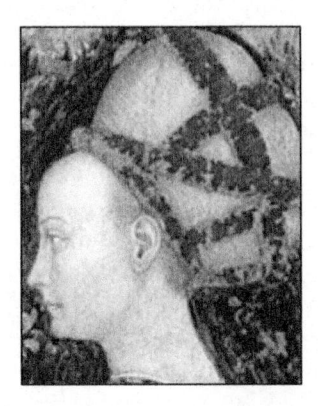

The princess he has saved is on the other side of the horse wearing a very ornate costume and a strangely bald forehead – it was the fashion at the time and the ladies of fashion shaved their heads to achieve it.

Behind all the people are the towers and palaces of Trebizond where the rescued princess came from. Trebizond was an ancient Christian kingdom on the Black Sea, ruled by descendants of the Byzantine Empire's royal family. Byzantine fell to the Ottoman Empire in 1453 but Trebizond held out for another decade. It was finally conquered by the Ottomans in the fifteenth century after a siege. It survives today as the city of Trabzon in Turkey.

Now take a look at the Presbytery which you will find just to the left of the Cavalli Chapel.

### Presbytery

On the left hand side is the tomb of Cortesia di Serego. Serego was a captain of Verona in the employ of the Scaligeri family, and here he is shown on his horse and ready for battle. A nice detail is the curtains which are being opened on either side of Serego on his horse.

Above Serego is a host of angels. Look carefully just to the right and below the angels and you will see a golden disc. The art experts say this is Serego rising up to join the angels. More fun are those who believe it's a depiction of a UFO!

*Map 4.5 - When you exit the church, take a look at San Giorgetto which stands on your right*

## San Giorgetto

The original church which stood here was named San Giorgetto. Later the Dominicans took over and rededicated it to Saint Pietro Martire who just happened to be a Dominican monk. However as often happens, the new name was never really adopted by the locals.

The church was funded in part by generous donations from Verona's wealthy citizens, and one of the most generous was Guglielmo da Castelbarco, a great friend of Cangrande II. His reward was the placement of his sarcophagus over the archway to the right of the church which was the entrance to the Monastery. The Scaliger family thought his tomb was very impressive so they used it as a prototype for their own sarcophagi in the Scaliger Tombs which you might already have visited. You can go through the archway to see some very old tombs in the old monastery grounds.

The church is deconsecrated now. If it's open do pop in to see some of the oldest frescoes in the city. The German knights who formed part of the army of Cangrande II were garrisoned in this area of Verona, and were given this church to worship in. They paid for some of the ancient frescoes you will see.

One of the most mysterious is The Unicorn Hunt.

**The Unicorn Hunt**

In the centre of this fresco is a unicorn with the Virgin Mary. It's thought to be a representation of the Annunciation. We see angels on both sides of Mary, God overseeing the occasion, and the baby Jesus descending towards Mary. But why is the Unicorn there? A popular theory is that it represents Mary's virginity since according to legend, only a virgin can tame a Unicorn.

*When you exit San Giorgetto stand with Santa Anastasia on your left. Opposite you stands the Hotel due Torri.*

# Mozart

Mozart was a child genius and his ambitious father dragged him around Europe to promote his skills.

He reached Verona in 1770 while on a tour of Italy and stayed in the Hotel due Torri. He gave two performances in Verona and the audience was clearly impressed, because in 1771 he was awarded membership of the Accademia Filarmonica of Verona.

## Heading to San Fermo Maggiore

Your next church is San Fermo Maggiore. If you follow the described route without stopping, you will get there in about 12 minutes. Obviously if you stroll there and take time to have a look at the sights en route, it will take a bit longer.

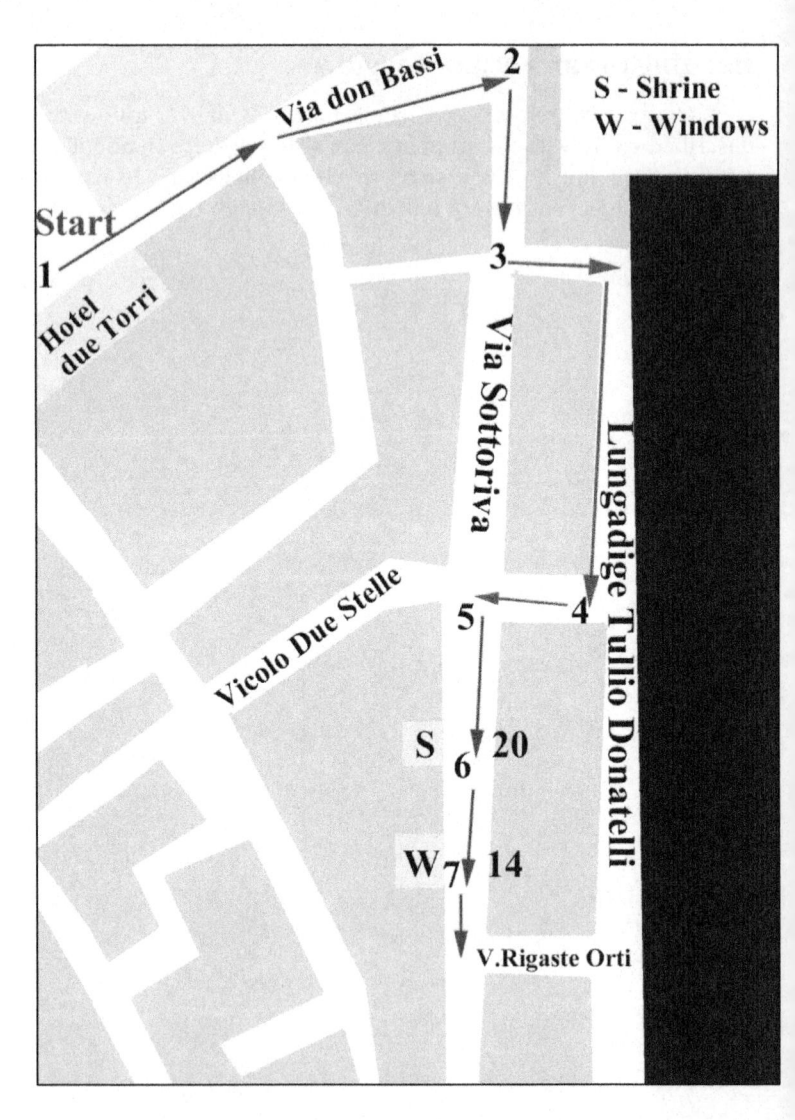

Map 5

***Map 5.1** - When you are ready to proceed, face the Hotel due Torre and turn left to retrace your steps along Via don Bassi.*

*Map 5.2 - At the end of the church you will reach Via Sottoriva where you turn right. Walk down to a zebra crossing just past number 42.*

*Map 5.3 - Turn left onto a tiny little street which will take you up to Lungadige Tullio Donatelli. Turn right to walk along this narrow riverside path.*

The riverside has been raised and strengthened with a long embankment. It holds back the worst that the Adige can bring, as no-one wants a repeat of the terrible floods which have swamped Verona in the past.

*Map 5.4 - After about 50 meters, turn right to return to Via Sottoriva, and then turn left to walk along it.*

## Via Sottoriva

This old street runs between two bridges and at one time was a hive of industry. Workmen loaded and unloaded goods from the river-boats. The street was lined with busy watermills and sawmills, some of which were swept away during a catastrophic river flood. It's very much quieter today.

A long arcade runs down the right-hand side of the street and it's very atmospheric to walk along under it. Long ago it was a very gloomy place at night and not the safest place to wander, but it's perfectly safe now.

*Map 5.5 - Walk along to number 7 which is under one of the arches – confusingly its opposite number 20!*

## Madonna and Child

You will see a little shrine to Mary and Jesus, and it is usually surrounded by flowers and candles so it's clearly popular.

The shrine was here during the great flood in the nineteenth century and it survived undamaged, which was deemed miraculous.

Beneath the image is a plaque which was placed there by Cardinal Canossa to mark the miracle. It states that if you say an

Ave Maria to the image, you are granted an indulgence of 100 days. So if you were unfortunate enough to end up in purgatory, your sentence before getting out would be reduced by 100 days.

***Map 5.6 - Continue along Via Sottoriva to number 14 and take a look at the building opposite it.***

This elderly building has beautiful Romanesque windows. The windows have a three-lobed arch at the top.

***Map 5.7 – Keep walking along Via Sottoriva and pass Vicolo Regaste Orti on your left.***

F - Fountain
P - Plaque

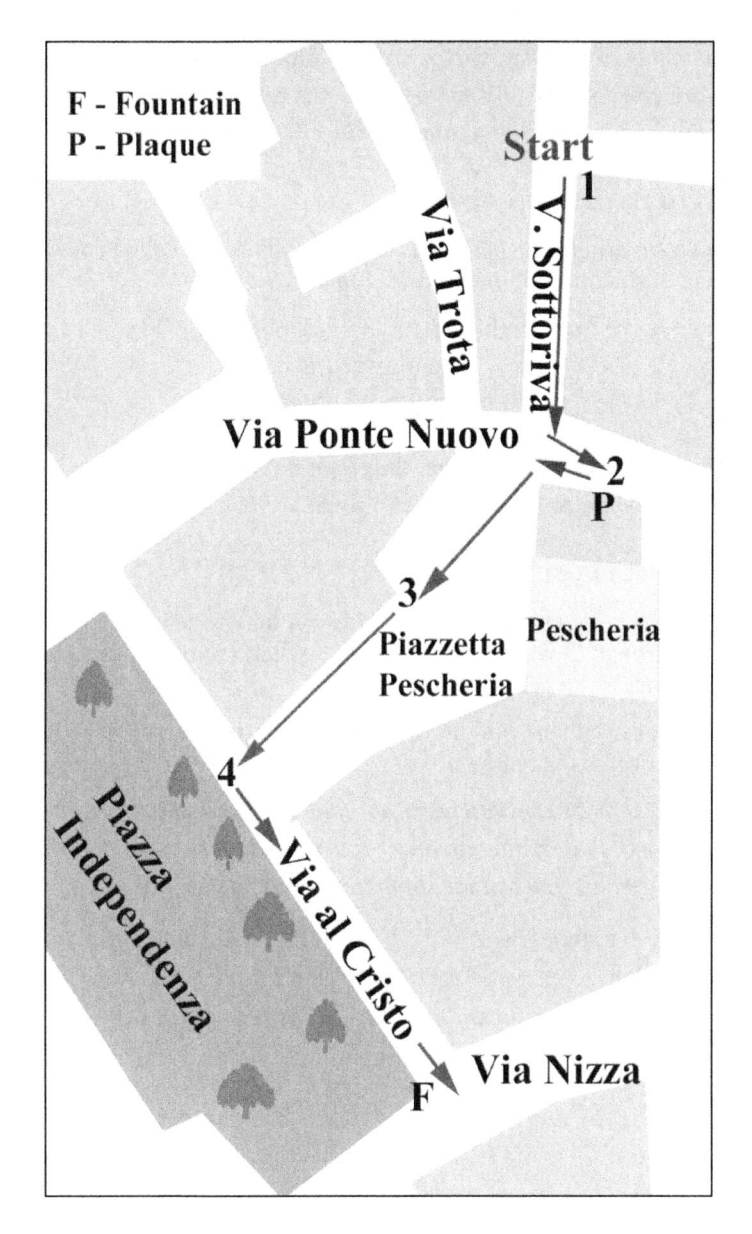

Map 6

*Map 6.1 - You will come to a junction with Via Ponte Nuovo.*

*You will be continuing straight ahead into Piazzetta Pescheria, but before you do, cross Via Ponte Nuovo and take a look at the plaque on the wall on your left at number 10.*

## Berto Barbarani Again

This is where the poet you read about in Piazza delle Erbe was born. His plaque commemorates him as:

> Born in this house - December 3, 1872
> to mortal life
> to immortal poetry

*Map 6.2 – Facing the plaque, turn right a few steps and then turn left into Piazzetta Pescheria, Fish Square.*

## Piazzetta Pescheria

This is a lovely old square and if you look to your left as you walk through it, you will see the old Pescheria with its crenelated roof. That is the old fish market.

It was originally built in the fifteenth century and amazingly it is still a well-used market.

*Map 6.3 - With the Pescheria on your left-hand side, follow the right hand side of the square. You will come to a wall with a gateway where you can see some trees peeping over the wall.*

Piazza Independenza sits behind the wall, which you may already have visited if you have done Walk 2.

*Map 6.4 - Turn left along little Via al Cristo to reach a T-junction with Via Nizza.*

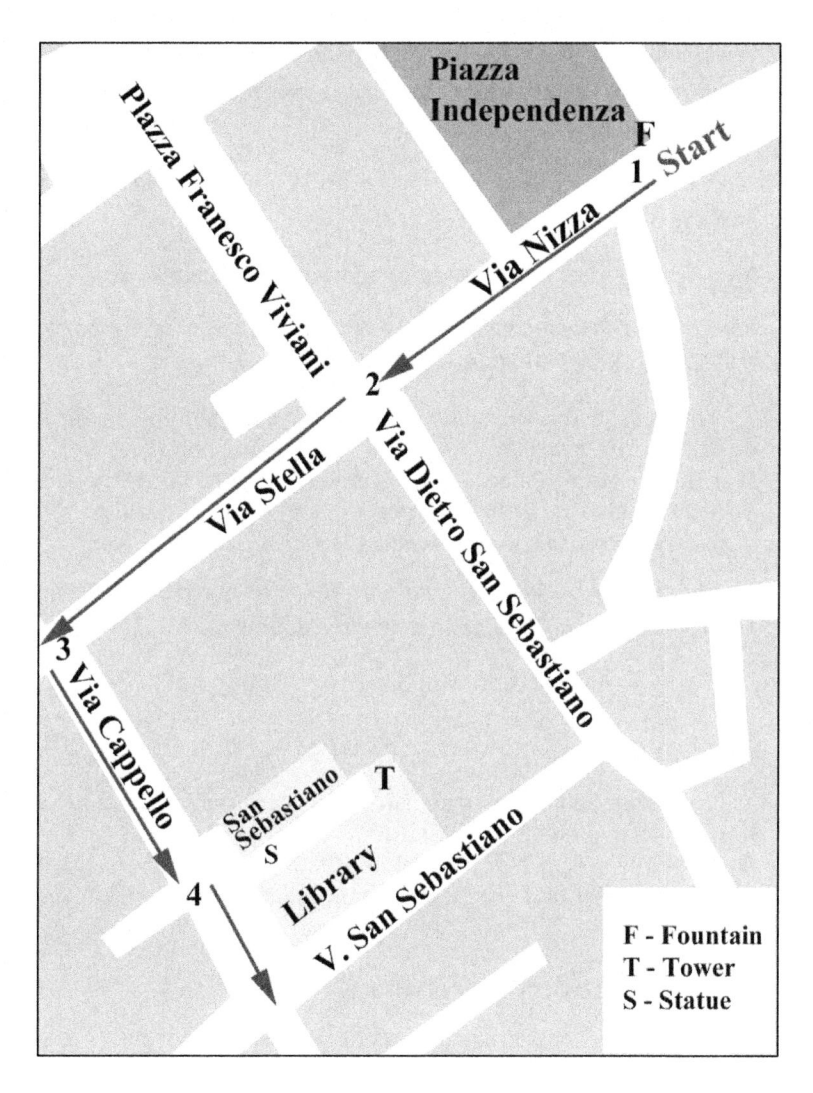

Map 7

***Map 7.1** - Turn right into Via Nizza, passing a flight of steps leading up to Piazza Independenza and a fountain on your right as you do so.*

*Walk along Via Nizza leaving Piazza Independeza behind. You will reach a crossroads where you can see the Torre Lamberti diagonally right.*

*Map 7.2 - With Via Nizza directly behind you, walk straight ahead into narrow Via Stella.*

*Map 7.3 - Turn left at the next crossroads into Via Capello.*

*Via Capello will widen out, and you will see two rather ugly modern buildings a bit further on at either side of the road.*

The reason for the widening of the road and the modern buildings is that this area was devastated by the bombs of World War II. The gothic Palazzo Bertani stood here but was destroyed. Verona decided to leave this open space as a memorial to the destruction Verona suffered during the war.

*Find number 43 on your left hand side as the road widens. You will see a small building emblazoned over the door with*

Antichi Archivi di Biblioteca Comunale

## San Sebastiano

This was San Sebastiano, an old church which became a library in the eighteenth century. Most of the church was destroyed in World War II by bombs, but if you stand between it and the modern building beside it you can see the steeple of the old church.

## The Civic Library of Verona

The modern building at its side was built to replace the destroyed library and to house the ancient manuscripts and books in a modern environment. However the design leaves a lot to be desired!

There is also a statue of Emilio Salgari, the writer of adventure stories who you read about on walk 2, fittingly placed between the old and the new library.

*Map 7.4 - Now stand so that you have San Sebastiano on your left. Walk straight ahead between the two modern buildings, staying on Via Cappello.*

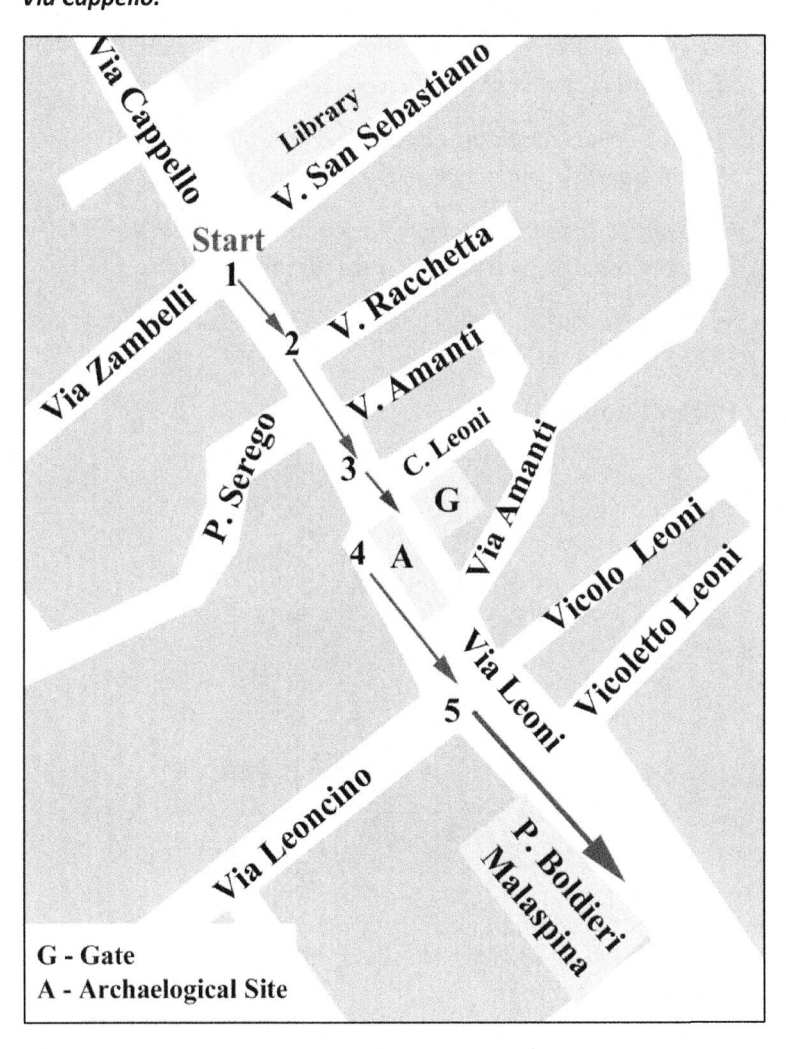

Map 8

*Map 8.1 - Once past the modern buildings, you will reach a crossroads with Vicolo San Sebastiano on your left and Via Zambelli on your right.*

*Cross over and keep to the left-hand side of Via Capella. You will see the tower of your next church ahead of you.*

*Map 8.2 – Pass Vicoletto Cieco Racchetta on your left, Piazzetta Serego your right, and finally and Vicolo Amanti on your left.*

*Map 8.3 - A few more steps will take you to a little street called Corticella Leoni on your left. On it stands the Porto Leoni.*

There are some handy Roman stones here if you need to sit down while you read.

## Porto Leoni

This is the second Roman gate which gave access through the city wall onto the Cardo Maximus, the main north-south road through the city.

No-one actually knows its original name. It got its current name due to a Roman sarcophagus which was found near here and which was decorated with two lions.

An urban legend has a more interesting explanation, it tells us that there was an underground passage from this gate to the arena, and it was how lions and other exotic animals were moved into the arena.

Quatuorviri were senior inspectors of Roman roads and gates, and there is an inscription between the columns which tells us the gate was under the jurisdiction of four Quatuorviri:

"P. VALERIVS / Q. CAECILIVS / Q. SER- VILIVS / P. CORNELIVS"

From the front you can look down to the street level the gate stood at all those centuries ago.

*Map 8.4 – With the gate on your left hand side, walk along Via Leoni.*

You can see an archaeological dig letting you see the foundations of the gateway and right at the end there is a nice section of Roman road.

*Map 8.5 - Once past the dig you will reach a crossroads with Vicolo Leoni and Via Leoncino. Keep straight, staying ahead on Via Leoni to reach a very pale pink building at number 10 on your right.*

## Palazzo Boldieri-Malaspina

This is the elderly Palazzo Boldieri-Malaspina which is very beautiful and at the time of writing is under restoration. It has gorgeous windows and an impressive archway.

The palace originally belonged to the Boldieri family who later sold it to the Malaspina family. It was threatened with demolition but has survived and perhaps when you are there, you will be able to visit.

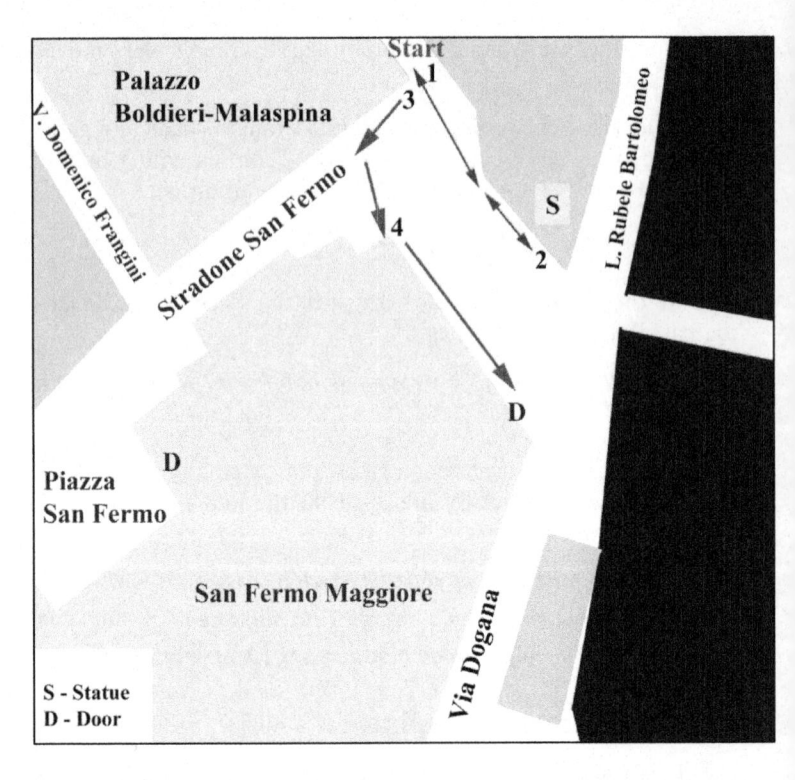

Map 9

***Map 9.1 - Walk past the palazzo to spot the church of San Fermo Maggiore on your right.***

***Before visiting it, find the statue of King Umberto I on your left. It stands in a little park.***

# King Umberto I

He was the son of Victor Emmanuell II, the first king of a United Italy.

He became deeply unpopular because of the Bava-Beccaris massacre in Milan. People were starving and came out to protest. The government responded by sending in the troops and many citizens were shot. Umberto had condoned the brutal government response and was assassinated two years later.

*Map 9.2 - Backtrack to reach the end of the Palazzo Bolieri-Malaspina again.*

*Map 9.3 - Carefully cross the road towards the church using the zebra crossings which you will find there.*

*Map 9.4 - Once over the crossings, walk along the front of the church to reach the left-hand side of the church which is near the riverside. That is where the tourist entrance lies.*

## San Fermo Maggiore

### Fermo and Rustico

The church is named after San Fermo. Fermo was a wealthy nobleman from the fifth century who was jailed because of his Christianity. Rustico was a relative who was also Christian and he chained himself to Fermo to show his support. The Roman councillor who in charge of the area, had them both decapitated just outside the Porta Leoni which you have just seen.

For some reason their remains were sent to Carthage in North Africa, but later were returned to Italy and to the city of Trieste. Four hundred years later the bishop of Verona requested that they should be returned to Verona, but he had to pay the ransom that Trieste demanded. When the saints were finally retrieved, their remains were placed in a small chapel on this spot.

The Benedictines arrived in the eleventh century and decided to build a church here, but they didn't want to disturb the saints' relics. So they first built a small church around the relics, and then built a much larger church above and around the first church.

In the thirteenth century the Franciscans arrived having coaxed the Pope to let them take over San Fermo church. They tried to evict the Benedictine monks still in residence, but they were having none of it and managed to stay at San Fermo for a further eleven years before finally leaving.

The Franciscans remodelled the upper church to the church you see today, and they moved the relics of the two saints upstairs into the main church in case of flooding. So this church is a bit like a layer cake, and as you go deeper, what you see gets older.

## Interior

The first thing which will hit you when you enter is the kaleidoscope of colour. The imposing roof which is like an upturned ship is decorated with an astonishing 416 saints. It was built by the Franciscans.

Walk down the nave to reach the main door which has a painting of the crucifixion above it. Turn right to find the Brenzoni family mausoleum which contains a beautiful work of art by two artists.

## Brenzoni Family Mausoleum

The central sculpture of the Resurrection is by Nanni di Bartolo, who was a pupil of Donatello. It has an eye-catching carved curtain being drawn back by the angels – very dramatic. At the bottom you can see the Roman soldiers who were napping. It has lost its original gold leaf decoration which would have made it even more dramatic.

The fresco which surrounds the sculpture is by Pisanello and is actually his first signed and dated work. It shows the Annunciation, with Mary receiving the news of her unexpected pregnancy on the right, and the archangel Gabriel who delivered the glad tidings on the left. The archangel Gabriel is particularly beautiful.

Now walk down the church to the left of the altar to find the Saint Anthony Chapel.

## Saint Anthony Chapel

In the fourteenth century this chapel was decorated with colourful frescoes. The Franciscans wanted to re-dedicate the church to Saint Anthony, so they just whitewashed it all over and decorated on top. Those additions have now been placed on movable panels which let you see the frescoes beneath them.

## The High Altar

The relics which took so much effort to get back to Verona are beneath the altar. Above them on the roof you will see some frescoes. No-one knows who did them but the experts think them so good that they gave the unknown artist a title, "The Master of the Redeemer".

## Dante Chapel

Face the High Altar and then take a look at the chapel on its right. That is the mausoleum of the last descendants of Dante Alighieri, the famous poet from Florence.

Make your way downstairs to the lower church. The stairway is on the left hand side of the Dante Chapel.

## Lower Church

This is a much older church and it's very atmospheric if there are not too many other tourists about. It is full of frescoes which all have a peculiar redness on the cheeks of the figures, as though they are all wearing rouge. The most famous are the frescos of the Virgin Mary nursing Jesus, and the Baptism of Christ by John the Baptist.

Take a look at the second column from the altar on your right-hand side – it has a date inscription which dates the church or at least that column at 1065.

You will also notice many images of a circle with a six petalled flower inside it. They are on the columns and ceiling. It is an ancient symbol of the resurrection which the Benedictine monks used.

When you reach the altar, take a look at the stone on the right hand side. That is thought to be the stone used in the decapitation of Fermo and Rustico.

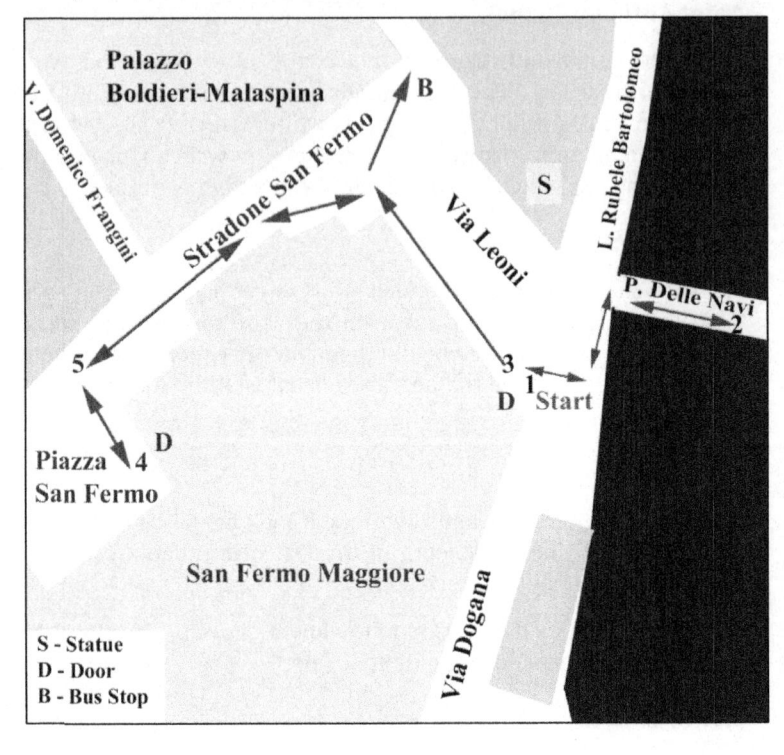

Map 10

***Map 10.1 - When you exit San Fermo, turn right to make your way onto the bridge, the Ponte Delle Navi.***

You can get a very good snap of the church from the bridge.

***Map 10.2 – Back-track to the church tourist entrance.***

***Map 10.3 – Stand with the church on your left. Walk along the back of the church and then turn left into Stradone San Fermo.***

***Walk along the side of the church to reach Piazza San Fermo and the front of the church.***

**San Fermo Doors**

It's worth the walk to see the bronze doors, as they tell you the story of Fermo and Rustico in a series of striking panels. The doors are actually quite modern as they were only added in 1997.

Take a look at the sarcophagus which sits to the left of the doors. That's the tomb of Avantino Fracastoro who was the doctor of the Scaliger family. There is another smaller niche on the right-hand side but it's empty.

## Getting to San Zeno

The last church on your itinerary is San Zeno. It is quite a distance away, so the best plan is to catch a bus.

*Map 10.4 - With the San Zeno main doors behind you, turn right to return to Stradone San Fermo.*

*Map 10.5 - Turn right to walk along Stradone San Fermo. You will pass Palazzo Boldieri-Malaspina on your left.*

*You will see some bus-stops. You can use your bus-map to select a route to get San Zeno.*

If it is Saturday you can catch number 30 which at the time of writing, will take you directly to San Zeno with no changes.

Otherwise you should catch a bus back towards Piazza Bra and change there to catch a bus to San Zeno.

Your exit stop for San Zeno is Piazza Corrubio.

***Very Important – Once you get on the bus, do check with the driver that he is going where you think he is going!***

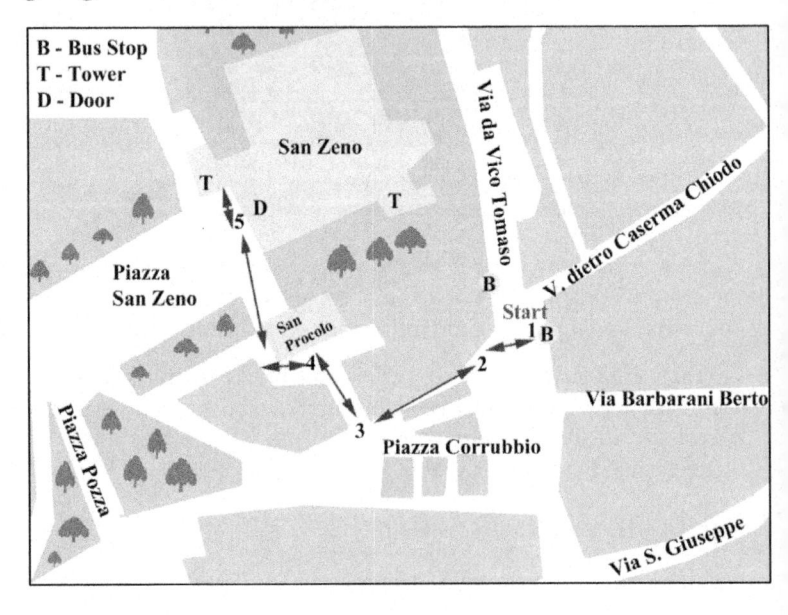

Map 11

From the bus-stop you can see the church tower across the road and to the right.

***Map 11.1 - There is no direct path to the church from the main road. To reach it from the bus-stop, cross the road and then walk into traingular Piazza Corrubio. The Piazza contains cafes, and trees on grassy islands on either side of the large entrance to an underground car-park.***

*Map 11.2 - Walk along the right-hand side of the piazza*

*Map 11.3 - Take the first right into Via San Procolo. Just ahead of you, you will see the church of San Procolo*

## San Procolo and Verona's Saints

The church was built in the tenth century on top of a huge Roman cemetery, but was badly damaged by the earthquake in the twelfth century and was later reconstructed.

The original crypt survived the earthquake and contains the tomb of San Procolo – he was the 4th saintly bishop of Verona. It's believed that the church also contains the tombs of Saints Euprepio, Cricino, and Agapito, the first three of Verona's bishops who all became saints.

The church was closed by Napoleon who suppressed many churches as he marched across Europe. After his defeat the church was badly neglected and eventually was near to collapse.

In 1985 it was saved by the Banca Popolare di Verona who paid to have it restored – but sadly the church is very rarely open.

*Map 11.4 - Follow the road as it wiggles round the church to bring you into the very large Piazza San Zeno.*

## Piazza San Zeno

On your right as you enter the square stands the church of San Zeno, with its belltower behind it. Standing next to San Zeno is a brick tower which belonged to the medieval monastery which once stood here.

## San Zeno

You might already have read about San Zeno if you visited San Zeno Oratorio on Walk 4.

He is the patron saint of Verona. He came to Verona from what was Mauretania and is now Algeria and Morocco. Since it's believed he was African, San Zeno is often depicted as black. He came to Verona in the fourth century as a monk and eventually became the eighth bishop.

**The Main Door**

A painting of the saint giving a blessing sits above the church main door.

The porch over the door is guarded by two lions, and the porch roof is held up by two telemons – columns with a little human figure at the top bearing the weight of the porch roof on his hands and shoulders.

Adam and Eve

Either side of the door is full of sculpture from the twelfth century. The panels depict various scenes from both the Old and New Testaments, such as Adam and Eve contemplating the snake and the infamous apple.

## The Hunt of Theodoric

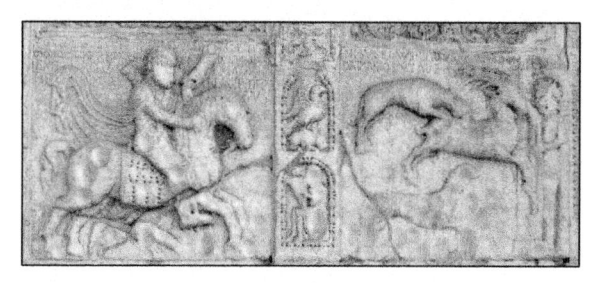

Theodoric the Great, who was King of the Ostrogoths in the sixth century, ruled a huge empire which included Italy.

There are many legends about his life and one of them is illustrated in the two bottom panels at the right-hand side of the main door.

One legend shows us King Theodoric hunting a stag with his hounds but the stag kept managing to evade them. Theodoric refused to give up and raced on and on, trying to catch it – and raced so far and so fast that he found himself at the gates of hell – where the devil was waiting for him!

## Wheel of Fortune

The window above the porch is a "Wheel of Fortune", which is the symbol of the goddess Fortuna. She spun her wheel and no-one knew if it would stop on something good or something bad, a bit like roulette.

*At the time of writing, the tourist entrance to the church is below the monastery tower.*

## Inside San Zeno

Here is another wonderful wooden church roof made to look like an upturned ship, this time decorated with stars.

Make your way down the church to the main wooden door where you can see 48 bronze panels. They mostly show key scenes from the bible but there are also some of the legends associated with San Zeno.

Take a look at the right-hand panel on the right-hand door, third row from the bottom. It shows San Zeno exorcising a demon from the daughter of Emperor Gallienus – with the demon floating above as it is disposed of.

With the door behind you, walk down the right-hand side of the church. You will pass an enormous painting of Saint Christopher with a very small Jesus on his shoulder. Stop when you reach a very unusual altar – it has two marble columns which look as though they have a knot in the middle. It's actually a porch from a fourteenth century church which was demolished long ago.

**The White Madonna**

On the right-hand side of the porch you will find an image of Mary and Jesus painted on a pilaster. It is called the White Madonna because of the unusual white robes which both Mary and Jesus are wearing.

## Upper church

Make your way up the steps to the upper church. Find a fresco of Saint George and the Dragon on you right-hand side – it's one of the oldest images in the church. The horse is remarkably calm considering the dragon has its tail wrapped around its legs.

At the end of the church is the altarpiece by Mantegna. You can see six paintings, but only the top three are the originals. Napoleon sent the entire altarpiece off to the Louvre and only the upper three sections were returned.

Mary and Jesus are surrounded by musical cherubs and framed with colourful fruits and rich drapery. Mary is attended by various saints. It's thought by the experts to be one of Mantegna's masterpieces.

To the left of the altar is a statue of San Zeno. Look closely and you will see that he is smiling which is very unusual for any church statue. Face away from the statue, and on your right you will see another huge painting of Saint Christopher.

Now descend the steps to the church again and take the steps down into the crypt.

## The Crypt

As you enter the crypt take a look at the arches at the entrance – they are very intricate with exotic creatures and vegetation. Descend into the crypt and into a forest of 49 columns, all slightly different from each other. This is where the remains of San Zeno lie in a bronze coffin. He is guarded by a decorative iron railing, very like the one which surrounds the Scaliger Tombs which you might already have seen on walk 2.

Return to the main church and walk down your right-hand side

## Cloister

You can visit the pretty cloister through the door way on you right.

The cloister and the brick tower which you saw in the Piazza are all that remain of the monastery which once stood here. The little porch you see protruding into the lawn was originally a washhouse for the monks of the monastery.

The columns which line the cloister are cut from red Verona marble, and the cloister holds various tombs of Verona's great families. As you walk around, look for a dark door with "Sacellum S. Benedicti" over it. That is where San Zeno was originally buried and later moved upstairs.

**Return to the church and turn right to complete the circuit.**

### Cup of San Zeno

As you approach the doors once more, you will see the Cup of San Zeno in the right-hand corner. It looks like a large baptismal font.

When Zeno exorcised the demon from the daughter of Emperor Gallienus, the Emperor was suitably grateful and wanted to give vast riches to Zeno. The bishop turned the riches down and instead requested a large stone basin. He then commanded the exorcised demon to carry the basin to Verona from Rome. The demon got a bit weary during his long march and dropped the basin and broke it. He turned up at Verona with only half a basin and was promptly ordered by San Zeno to go back and pick up the missing half. The demon complied and the two halves were joined together.

**When you exit the church you have completed this walk.**

**Map 11.5 - To return to town, stand with the San Zeno main door behind you and turn left to walk into Via San Procolo. Follow it around the church of San Procolo and back onto Piazza Corrubbio.**

**Turn left to reach the main road once more. Turn left and you should find the bus-stop just a few steps away.**

You have now reached the end of this walk.

# Walk 4 – Palaces and the Museum

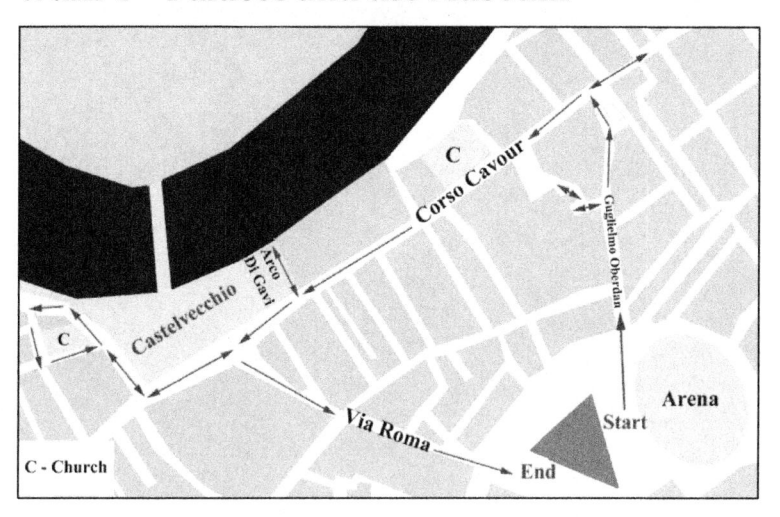

Overview Walk 4

This walk will take you from the Arena down to the riverside.

En route you will find remnants of the Roman period, many beautiful palazzos, the Castle which now houses a very good museum, and finally return to the Arena.

M - Memorial
S - Statue
F - Fountain
D - Door

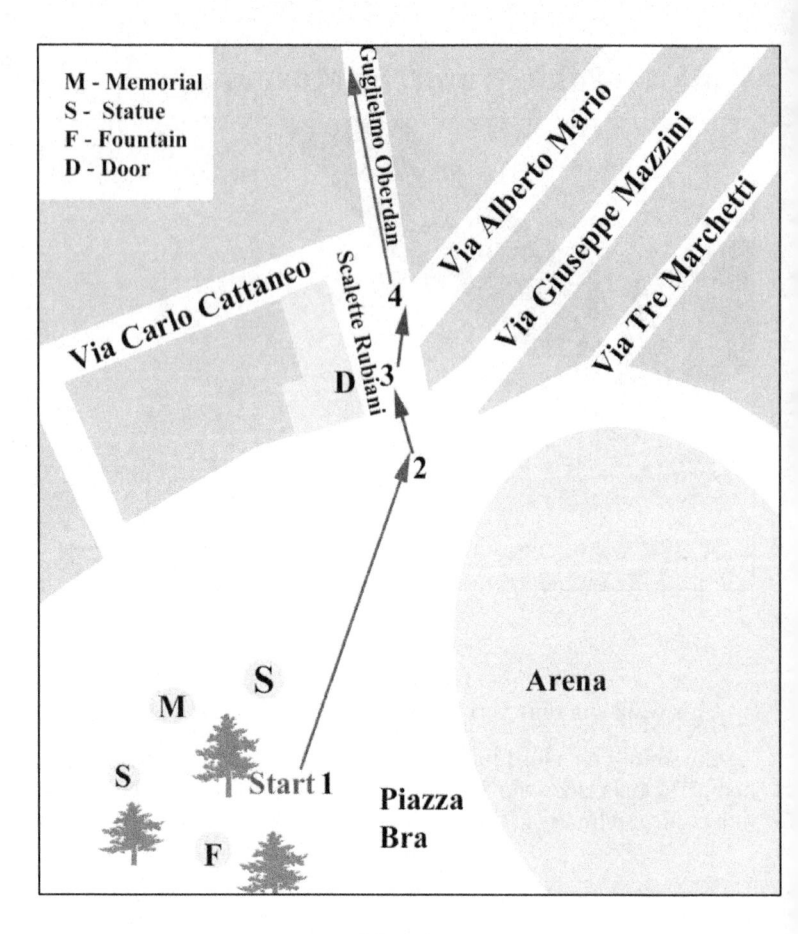

Map 1

This walk starts in Piazza Bra.

***Map 1.1 - Stand between the Arena and the tree-filled garden and face the Arena.***

***Turn left and start to skirt around the arena. You will soon see a junction of streets ahead of you.***

***Map 1.2 - Walk into the first street which is called Piazzetta Scalette Rubiani. It has a stone balcony on the right hand corner and an iron railing balcony on the left hand corner.***

122

*Once in the Piazzetta you will see an ornate door on your left – it has the words Societa Letteraria above it.*

## Literary Society

Verona's Literary Society started in 1808 when thirteen of the city's intellectuals decided the people of Verona needed somewhere to gather, discuss, and most importantly to read.

The library has books from as far back as the sixteenth century which are very precious, gathered by its enthusiastic founders and members.

The society has survived the tumult of the Wars of Independence and two World Wars. Many of Italy's best minds have been members, including Aleardo Aleardi, a poet whose statue you will see later on this walk.

Anyone can apply to join and if accepted can use the reading room to enjoy the books and publications gathered inside. There are frequent discussions and talks on all sorts of topics, and it hosts concerts and plays throughout the year.

*Map 1.3 – With the Literary Society on you left-hand side, take a few steps straight ahead to reach a fork in the road.*

*Map 1.4 - Take the left hand fork which is called Via Guglielmo Oberdan. Pass Via Carlo Cattaneo on your left.*

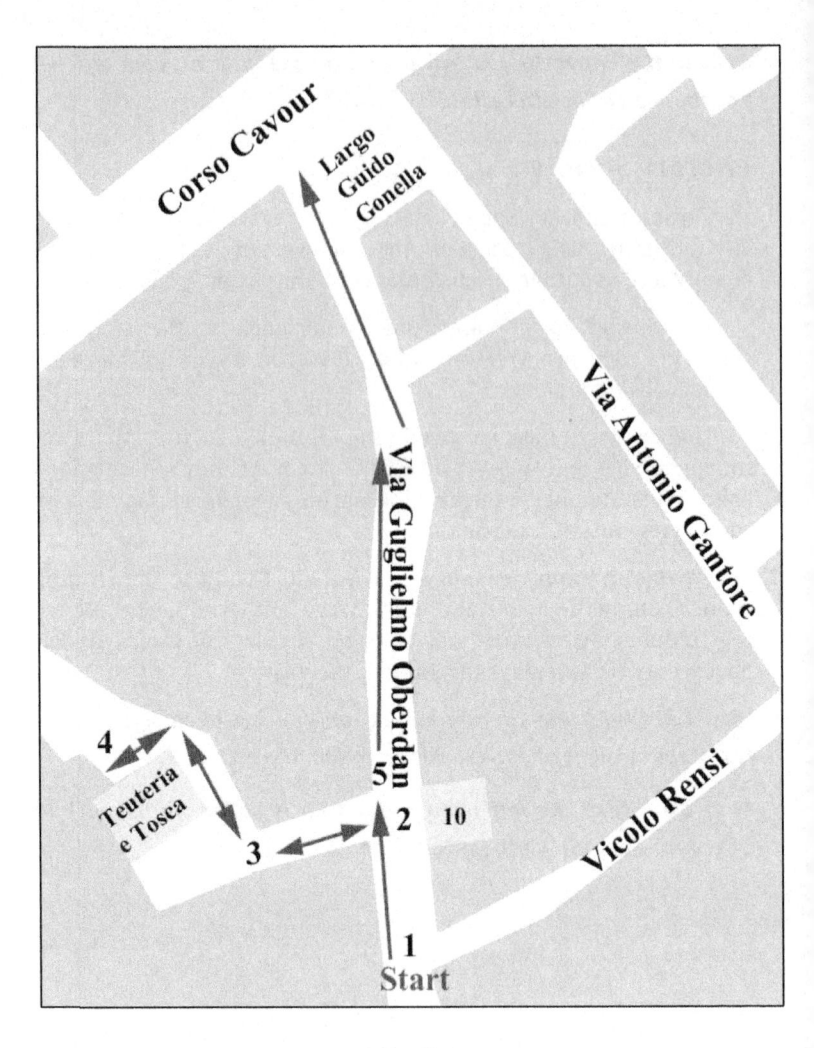

Map 2

*Map 2.1 - Follow Via Guglielmo Oberdan and pass Vicolo Rensi on your right. A few more steps will bring you to number 10 on your right-hand side. It has a large arched wooden doorway.*

*Map 2.2 - Take a little detour by going along the unnamed little street opposite the door.*

*It will take you into a tiny square with a very old church on your right which is dedicated to Sante Teuteria e Tosca. The little church is attached to the much larger church you can see behind it.*

*Map 2.3 - Turn right to walk around the little church to reach its door.*

## Sante Teuteria e Tosca

It was built in the 5th century near the Via Postumia.

### Teuteria and Tosca

Teuteria and Tosca are two female saints who were buried here. Princess Teuteria came from a wealthy Anglo-Saxon family and became a Christian, however she was pursued by a pagan nobleman called Osvaldo who wouldn't take no for an answer. She had to flee to Italy to escape him and took refuge with the female hermit Tosca in her cave.

Osvaldo followed her but his men found they couldn't get into the cave because spiders had spun such a thick sticky web that it was impossible to pass. The ladies lived in the cave for the rest of their lives and died only a few days apart. They were buried here and when this little church was built by a wealthy local family, the bones of the two saints were dug up and placed inside the church.

Like many churches in Verona it takes a long lunchbreak, but if you are lucky enough to find the door open, pop in.

### Inside the church

Descend the steps into a small but very atmospheric church. During excavations the diggers discovered mosaics, human bones, and a Roman floor beneath the one you are standing on now – so it's thought that this was originally a Roman burial site.

The altar has three carvings, the lady on the left is Teuteria, the one on the right is Tosca, and the Virgin Mary sits in the middle.

This little church became the Bevilacqua family chapel - you will see the Bevilacqua family palazzo soon. The tomb on the right side of the altar holds Francesco Bevilacqua, and on the wall above it is a little figure of Jesus with carvings of the sun and the moon beneath him. Opposite Francesco's tomb is another family tomb, this time of the three Bevilacqua brothers Giovanni, Antonio, and Gregorii.

The church font was cut from one piece of marble in the thirteenth century, and this is still a popular place for baptisms with family and friends gathered around it.

*Map 2.4 - With the door of the church behind you, turn right and back-track around the church and then turn left to return down the little unnamed street into Via Guglielmo Oberdan.*

*Map 2.5 - Turn left to continue down Via Guglielmo Oberdan. The road will curve left and eventually you will pop out onto busy Corso Cavour.*

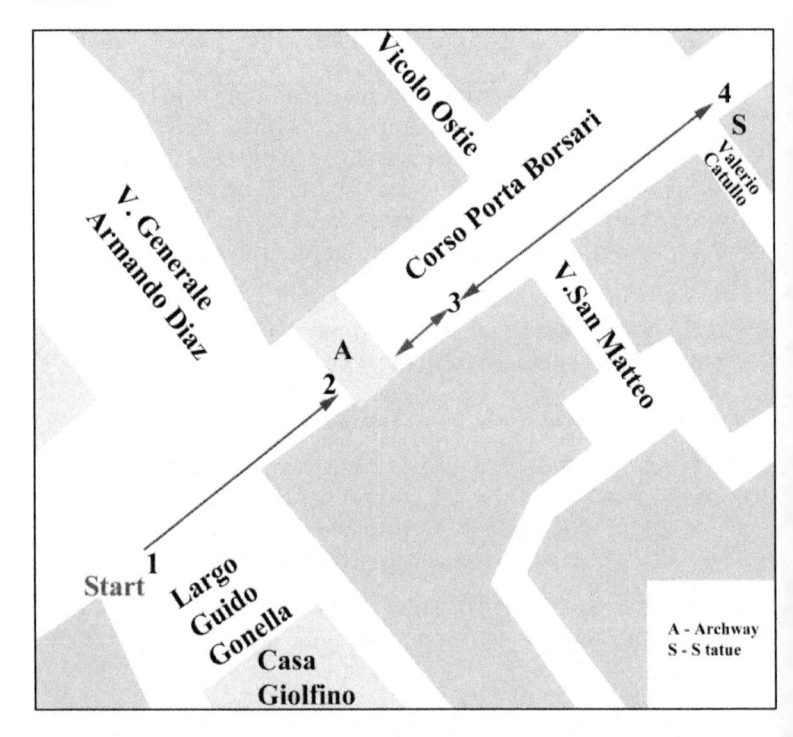

Map 3

*Map 3.1 - Turn right to reach the Porta dei Borsari.*

## Porta dei Borsari

This is one of two surviving gates through the city wall which were built by the Romans. Verona is naturally protected on three sides by the loop of the river Adige, so the Romans only had to build a wall across the southern edge of the town to secure it. The Porta dei Borsari was built in the 1st century where the very important Via Postumia entered Verona.

The Romans originally named the gate Porta Iovia, after a temple to the god Jupiter which once stood nearby.

This side of the gate is the most ornate, as it was built to impress visitors to the city - it has four Corinthian columns bordering the two archways.

If you look above the arches you can see an inscription which tells us that the city's walls were restored in 265 AD by Emperor Gallienus. The inscription would have been formed of bronze letters, but the valuable bronze lettering was removed long ago leaving us with just the marks left behind on the stone.

Much later in the Middle Ages, the gate was renamed as Porta dei Borsari, Gate of the Purse Holders. Verona imposed a tax on goods entering the city which was collected by customs guards stationed here.

*Map 3.2 - Face the gate and step through one of the archways into what was Roman Verona.*

## Roman Roads

Roman cities were mostly built following the same pattern. Two main roads crossed the city, the Cardo Maximus which ran north to south, and the Decumaus Maximus which ran east to west. They were very important roads which were built with the best materials, and the city's most important buildings were built along them.

You are now standing at the start of the Decumaus Maximus which led to the important Piazza delle Erbe which you may already have explored on Walk 2. The other main Roman road, the Cardo Maximus, is found on Walk 3.

*Map 3.3 - With the plainer side of the gate now behind you, walk straight ahead. Pass Vicolo San Matteo on your right and then stop at the next right hand street, Via Valerio Catullo.*

## Medusa

On the side of the corner building is a striking carving taken from a Roman sarcophagus and incorporated into this building.

It's thought to be Medusa. Look at the side of the stone to see another carving, this time of Triton, the son of Poseidon and Aphrodite, who is playing a musical instrument called a bucina.

*Map 3.4 - Backtrack towards the gate and pass through it once more. Corso Cavour now stretches out in front of you.*

## Corso Cavour

Corso Cavour follows the route of the Via Postumia and is one of Verona's oldest streets. The Romans were fond of burying important people along the sides of the main roads leading into their cities, which explains the various tombs which have been found along this street.

Later it became the most fashionable place to live, so you will see a line of sumptuous palazzos as you walk down it.

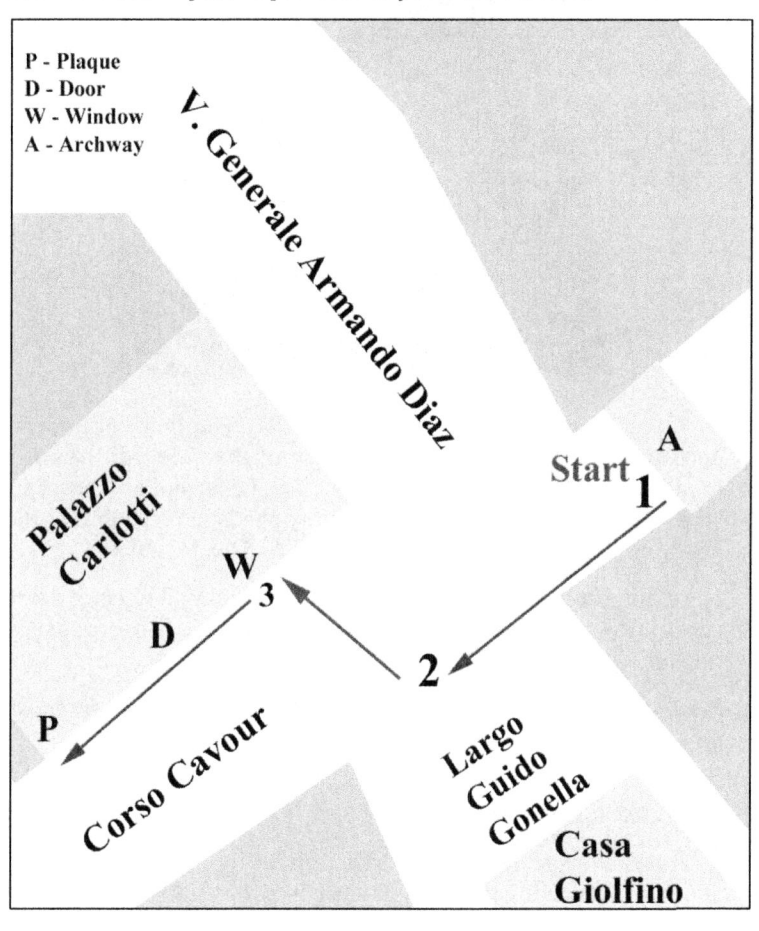

P - Plaque
D - Door
W - Window
A - Archway

Map 4

*Map 4.1 - A few steps along Corso Carvour will bring you to a little square on your left-hand side. It is called* Largo Guido Gonella, *and at the back of the square is the Casa Giolfino.*

129

## Casa Giolfino

If you've already done walk 2 you have read that Verona was once called the "painted city" because of the colourful frescoes found on so many of the buildings. The Casa Giofino shows us some remnants which were painted by the artist Nicolo Giolfino and his much more famous artist friend Andrea Mantegna.

At the time of writing the frescoes are really in need of some restoration, so hopefully Verona will not let them deteriorate any further.

*Map 4.2 - On the opposite side of Corso Cavour stands the much larger Palazzo Carlotti. Cross over to reach it.*

## Palazzo Carlotti

It has an ornate door with a balcony held up by four columns, and has five windows at ground level on either side of the door.

Look at the second window to the right of the door. You will see that the stone below the window is a different colour from the other windows. Look carefully to see a piece of old graffiti on that stone which translates as:

> 1710, on the day of the prize
> I Jacometo of Patulia was Sergeant here.

Long ago Verona held an annual series of races called the Palio. There were four races, for horsemen, donkeys, male runners, and even one for women but they were only allowed to walk! The winners were awarded a piece of cloth which was dyed a different colour for each race.

The race passed this point, and this graffiti was put here by Sergeant Jacometo on the day of the 1710 Palio – it's a kind of ancient "I was here" marker.

Dante added a verse about the race in his Divine Comedy:

> Then he turned round, and seemed to be of those
> who at Verona run for the green cloth across the
> plain; and seemed to be among them the one
> who wins, and not the one who loses

Verona's Palio was stopped by Napoleon when he ruled the city; he wanted to avoid any event which caused crowds to gather in case of rebellion. It's surprising that Verona has not resumed it as a means of drawing more tourists in – Siena still runs its Palio and it is a huge success.

*Map 4.3 - Now walk past the ornate doorway to the end of the Palazzo.*

## Tybalt and Romeo

Here you will find a plaque which marks the supposed spot where the duel between Romeo and Tybalt took place.

If you look closely you can see the arches of Porta dei Borsari in the background.

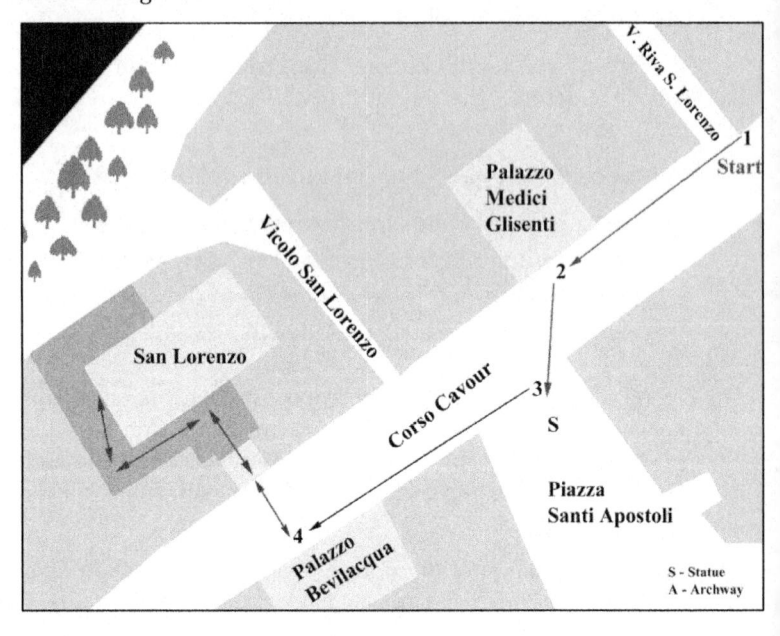

Map 5

***Map 5.1 - Walk further along Corso Cavour to number 10 on the right-hand side. This is the Palazzo Medici Glisenti.***

## Palazzo Medici Glisenti

This palazzo is about a hundred years older than the Palazzo Carlotti being built in the fifteenth century.

Its upper windows are flanked by twirling columns and topped with intricate carvings – which are said to be Venetian in style.

***Map 5.2 - A little further on the left-hand side of Corso Cavour is a statue.***

# Aleardo Aleardi

Aleardi was a poet from Verona who lived through the traumatic period of the Wars of Independence.

He had a memorable name, but perhaps wrote less memorable poems. They did however land him in trouble with the authorities, as they were political and supported Italy's battle for independence from Austria. He ended up in prison twice because of his writings, and Austria finally threw him out of the country altogether.

Once Austria was itself ousted, Aleardi returned to Verona and became its representative in the new Italian government. This statue was put up the year Aleardi died.

Around its base are some inscriptions part of which roughly translated says:

> His songs revived in the young the love of Italy
> that drew them to the glory of the homeland battles

***Map 5.3 - Continue along Corso Cavour and a little further down on your left-hand side at number 19 is the Palazzo Bevilacqua.***

## Palazzo Bevilacqua

This belonged to the Bevilacqua family who you read about in the Santa Teuteria e Tosca church earlier.

The Bevilacqua were a very important Veronese family – they made their fortune in the timber market and Francesco Bevilacqua later became an advisor to Cangrande II. The family commissioned Sanmicheli, the most famous architect from Venice, to design and build their palace - and he did not disappoint.

Beneath the ground floor windows is a line of supporting lions. Look above the windows on the ground floor to see the busts of famous Romans – Julius Caesar guards the main door! Further up is a line of very unusual spiral columns. When the family died out, the last Duchess Bevilacqua bequeathed the palace to Verona.

*Map 5.4 – Cross Corso Cavour to reach a very pretty archway.*

## San Lorenzo

San Lorenzo stands over the archway to welcome you in. He is holding a grating in his hand - it represents the grill he was barbequed over, which was definitely one of the more unpleasant ways to achieve sainthood. He is said to have told his tormentors:

"I'm done on this side, turn me over"

He became the patron saint of cooks and chefs.

Once through the archway you will enter a little garden with an old well. The church appears immediately different as it is built of alternating tiers of tuff and brick, which gives it a very distinctive pattern.

The church stands on another old Roman site – this time a temple to Venus. San Lorenzo was built at the start of the twelfth century but was damaged in the great earthquake of 1117. It was enlarged while it was repaired, and you can see that the lower levels are made of different materials to the upper levels which were added.

Before you go in, walk around to the front to see the two cylindrical towers on either side of the main door. This church is unusual because it has three upper galleries where the women would go to worship – they entered by those towers

Inside the church you will find a striped stone pattern. Look up to see the women's' galleries. The unusual segregation of worshippers went a step further - there were separate galleries for maidens, widows, and matrons.

There is one art work you should find.

Above the altar is a work by Domenico Brusasorci who came from Verona. His painting shows us the Madonna and Child, John the Baptist, Saint Lawrence (of course) and Saint Augustine.

Brusasorci was trained by his father but became much more successful and was one of the leading artists in Verona. He introduced Mannerism to Verona – which uses very dramatic figures where proportion and balance are exaggerated, producing paintings that seem very elegant if also very unnatural.

*Map 5.5 - Exit the church and return through the archway. Cross the street once more.*

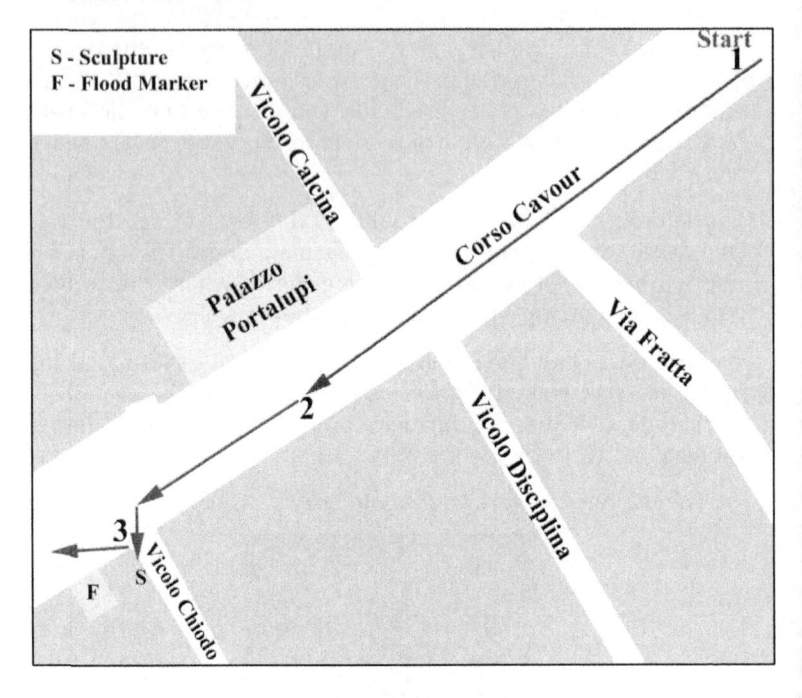

Map 6.1

*Map 6.1 - Turn right to continue along Corso Cavour.*

*Pass Via Fratta and Vicolo Disciplina on your left. On your right at number 38 you will see the Palazzo Portalupi. It's the one with "Banco D'Italia" above the door.*

## Palazzo Portalupi

This was the home of the Portalupi family – who were successful and wealthy lawyers.

A Roman bust watches over you from above the door as you approach. Above him is a line of columned windows – with two angels on top of the middle one.

Above the angels are smaller windows, each guarded by more female figures. Centre stage is a large clock guarded by two wolves, which feature on the Portalupi coat of arms.

*Map 6.2 - Walk a few steps further along to reach Vicolo Chiodo on your left. Just at the corner of Vicolo Chiodo you will see a small sculpture of a young woman's head on the wall.*

## Isolina

That is Isolina who lived in Vicolo Chiodo at number 9 at the start of the twentieth century.

She had a relationship with a soldier billeted in Verona and became pregnant. The soldier and his buddies decided the best solution was to abort the baby themselves – which they immediately attempted to do by force. It ended in disaster as Isolina died. Her body was cut up and thrown into the river but was washed up and found by some washer-women. The townspeople were incensed but the army closed ranks around their men and no further action was taken. Nothing remains of her story except this little face in stone.

*Map 6.3 – Take a few more steps along Corso Cavour, and at number 37 you will find a flood marker near the ground.*

## Flood marker

Verona has always suffered floods – an obvious danger to any city built by the riverside.

Northern Italy experienced torrential rainfall in September 1882 which caused the waters of the Adige to rise and rise. Finally the river broke its banks and 70% of Verona was flooded. Mills which lined the river banks were uprooted by the teeming waters and carried down the river, bridges collapsed, and people died.

As the flood subsided King Umberto II travelled to Verona from Rome to give support and comfort to the homeless and the bereaved. It was after that flood that Verona started to build walls and levees along the riverside.

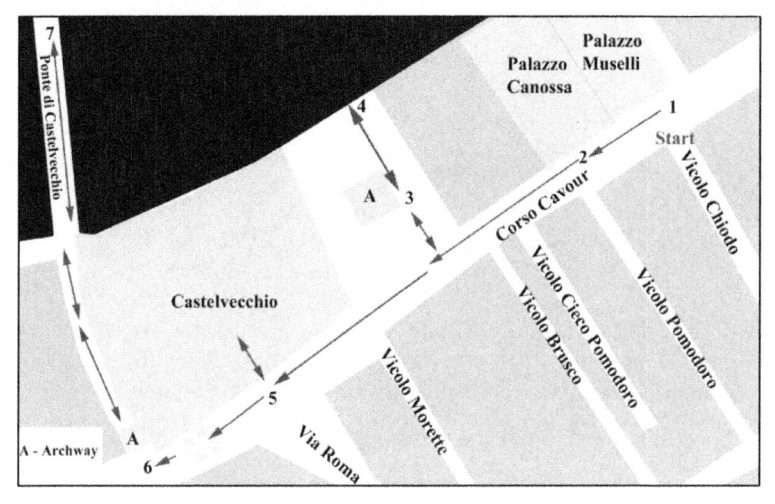

Map 7

***Opposite the flood marker stands the Palazzo Muselli.***

# Palazzo Muselli

The Muselli family at one time had a fantastic art collection housed in their palazzo, works by Titian, Veronese, Bellini, Bruegel, Cranach, Parmigianino and even Michelangelo. Sadly over the years it has all been sold off, mostly to museums in Europe.

So today, the most notable feature of the palace is its three chimneys – which are rather handsome. If you look closely you can see that each chimney is built as a medieval castle.

*Map 7.1 – Facing the Palazzo turn left to continue along Corso Cavour. You will reach Palazzo Canossa which sits on your right-hand side at number 44*

## Palazzo Canossa

This palace was also designed by Michele Sanmicheli from Venice. It looks much simpler than the ornate Palazzo Bevilacqua you saw a little while ago, until you look up.

Above the second row of small windows is a wonderful line of running dogs – dogs appear in the coat of arms of the Canossa family. Look right up to the roof and there we have a line of Gods. Across the top you will see an inscription which translates as:

> And their children and their seed will live on forever

The palace survived the bombs of World War II but only just. The far left window grill is still bent – caused by a nearby bomb explosion.

*Map 7.2 - Continue along Corso Cavour and turn right into a little square to find the Arco del Gavi.*

## Arco dei Gavi

This arch was built by the Gavi family, another wealthy family from Verona. It was originally built outside the original city walls on the Via Postumia. Later when Verona expanded and the new city wall was built, this arch was incorporated into it.

Originally those empty niches held statues of the family, but they haven't survive. We know the architect was Lucio Vitruvio Cerdone, who was a Greek slave who was freed by a Roman citizen. His name is inscribed on the inner side of one of the pillars.

*L. CERDO ARCHITECTVS*

Time hasn't been kind to the arch. By the middle ages it was mostly below street level with some huts leaning against it. Napoleon then had it demolished to clear the road, so his cannon and other large pieces of artillery could get into Verona easily. Fortunately the stones were stashed in the arena, and Mussolini later had it rebuilt close to its original site as part of his grand plan to restore Italy to its power during Roman times.

Sadly the arch is still not safe as it's a target for vandals, so nowadays it is under constant video surveillance.

*Map 7.3 - Walk past the arch to the end of the square to reach the riverside and look left.*

## Ponte di Castelvecchio

You will reach the bridge shortly, but you get a very good view of it from here. When it was built it had the world's largest arch span.

*Map 7.4 - Backtrack past the arch once more to return to Corso Cavour.*

*Turn right and the much older building coming up on your right is the Castelvecchio itself, the "Old Castle". Make your way to the entrance, which is just a few steps along.*

## Castelvecchio

It was Big Dog II who had this castle built in the fourteenth century, and it's very utilitarian as it was meant for defence. It even had a moat, which is of course now dry.

It guards the bridge over the Adige which would have given the Scaligeri family an escape route to the north if Verona was attacked by any of its many rivals to the south. Much later Napoleon stayed here when he visited Verona. It remained as a military building until the twentieth century, but it now houses the Castelvecchio Museum.

Be warned, there is no café in this museum despite the obvious amount of income it would generate. So you might want to pop into a nearby establishment first for a refreshment and use of their facilities before tackling the museum. Also it's a large museum, so if you are interested in art, bank on spending at least an hour there, probably two.

## Museo di Castelvecchio

The Museo di Castelvecchio is where Verona placed its greatest art works.

The museum had a very lax security system in place. Just a few years ago, it allowed six of the most famous and interesting paintings to be stolen. Luckily they were recovered from The Ukraine a year later, and have been repaired and are on display once again.

Here are some highlights to look out for:

### Saint Catherine of Alexandria

Here is Saint Catherine again – still holding her wheel. This statue is from the fourteenth century.

## Cangrande on his horse

If you have already visited the Scaliger Tombs on Walk 2 you will have seen where this statue originally stood. Here you can see Cangrande's smiling face much more clearly.

## Madonna of the Quail - Pisanello

This is the absolute best in the museum, it's simply beautiful. The Virgin Mary is being crowned by two angels and surrounded by various birds, including the quail which gives the painting its name – it's the large bird in the foreground.

**Madonna del Roseto - Michelino da Besozzo or Stefano da Verona**

It's the colours which will draw you to this painting of The Madonna which dates from the fifteenth century.

She sits in a garden fenced by roses and the fence represents her virginity. Accompanying her is Saint Catherine of Alexandria who is sitting on a wooden wheel which she was tortured on. That's where we get Catherine Wheels for fireworks displays. Jesus seems very comfortable lying sucking his finger.

According to Christian belief peacocks are incorruptible, so there are few of them in the garden too.

**Contesa tra le Muse e le Pieridi - Tintoretto**

The Pierids were nine sisters who challenged the nine Muses to a singing contest. They lost and were turned into magpies in retribution. Here Tintoretto shows us the Muses still singing together while the Pierids are now magpies and flying off clutching their sheet music and instruments.

**Portrait of a Child with a Drawing – Caroto**

The young boy in this painting is proudly showing you his drawing; it is amusing to think of the artist painting a drawing by a child. The art experts tell us he didn't quite manage it as the stick-man's left eye is far too accomplished for a child.

### La Pala Bevilacqua-Lazise - Veronese

This painting was commissioned by the Bevilacqua-Lazise family and they asked a very young Veronese to take it on.

As usual the family members are placed in the painting, kneeling at the bottom in prayer. It's a sort of early selfie if you think about it. Above them sits the Virgin Mary with Jesus, a couple of angels, and two saints.

The right hand saint who is a bishop is especially interesting because of his twisted position to look behind him, which makes you look at what he is looking at. His golden robes are also eye-catching.

*Map 7.5 - When you exit the castle, turn right along Corso Cavour towards the end of the castle.*

As you do, you will see reach a clock tower on your right.

## Arco dei Gavi again

On the road beside the tower you will find four marks on the cobblestones. They pinpoint where the Arco dei Gavi originally stood.

On the clock tower is a small plaque under a much larger plaque. It commemorates the history of the arch and translates as:

HERE YOU CAN FIND THE CENOTAFIO
CALLED ARCO DEI GAVI
ERECTED IN THE GOLDEN CENTURY OF ROME
DEMOLISHED BY THE FRENCH IN THE YEAR MDCCCV

*Map 7.6 – Just beyond the clock tower, turn right through an archway and you will eventually emerge onto the Ponte di Castelvecchio.*

## Ponte di Castelvecchio

Walk at least halfway over the bridge and admire its battlements. As already mentioned it was built in the fourteenth century and stood more or less intact until the German Army retreated from Verona in 1945. They blew it up along with all the other bridges over the Adige.

Verona decided to rebuild the lost bridges and in 1945 hauled the stones from the riverbed. Then in 1949 they started to rebuild. They put as many stones back in their original positions as possible. Those which had been completely destroyed were replaced by extracting similar blocks from the original quarry in San Giorigo di Vapolicella.

On the other side of the river is a park which contains the Arsenal. It was built by the Austrians but it's not open to the public as yet, so it's of limited interest.

*Map 7.7 - When you want to move on, backtrack across the bridge and go through the archway once more to return to Corso Cavour.*

If it's a Saturday you could visit the San Zeno in Oratorio church, as that's the only day its open. If that doesn't interest you or if it's not Saturday, continue this walk from "Back Into Town" on Page 152.

# To San Zeno in Oratorio

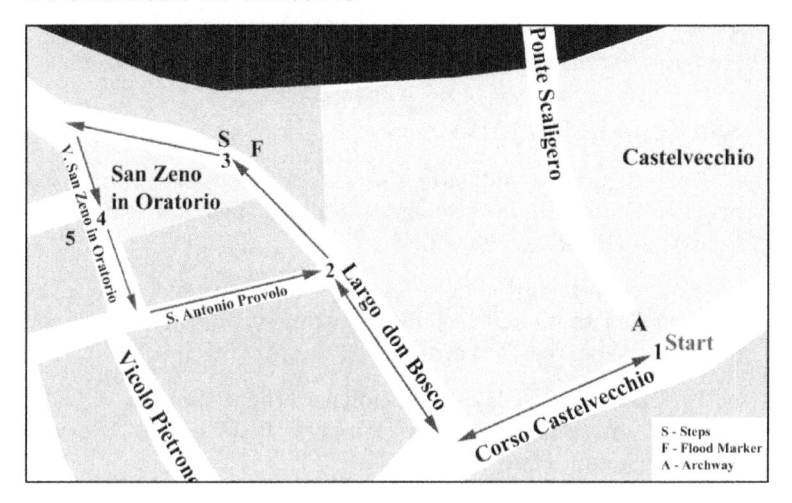

Map 8

*Map 8.1 - To reach the church, stand with the Ponte di Castelvecchio archway behind you and turn right to walk along Corso Castelvecchio.*

*Take the first right down Largo Don Bosco.*

You will get another view of the crenellated walls of Castelvecchio on your right-hand side as you do.

*Map 8.2 - Pass Stradone Antonio Provolo on your left.*

*As the road starts to bend left, you will see an old stone building on your left-hand side. That is the church.*

*But before proceeding, spot a little flight of steps up to the embankment on your right. Look just to the right of the steps. You can find two more flood-markers.*

# More flood markers

The top one marks the disastrous flood of 1882; the bottom one marks a less devastating flood of 1868.

*Map 8.3 - Now follow the church wall and take the first left into Vicolo San Zeno in Oratorio. You will reach the church entrance on the left – it is guarded by two saints and sits opposite number 5.*

## San Zeno in Oratorio

This is a very old site; the experts think a church was originally built here in the eighth century at the crossroads of the Via Postumia and the Via Gallica.

The church has been flooded and knocked down by earthquakes, so it's been rebuilt a few times since then. What you see now is from the 14th century.

In an ancient religious document, "The Dialogues of Saint Gregory", there is a mention of a river flood while Zeno was preaching in this church.

> "and though the church doors were open, yet did it not enter in. At last it grew so high, that it came to the church windows, not far from the very roof itself, and the water standing in that manner, did close up the entrance into the church, yet without running in: as though that thin and liquid element had been turned into a sound wall.
>
> And it fell so out, that many at that time were surprised in the church, who not finding any way how to escape out, and fearing lest they might perish for want of meat and drink, at length they came to the church door, and took of the water to quench their thirst, which, as I said, came up to the windows, and yet entered not in; and so for their necessity they took water, which yet, according to the nature of water, ran not in: and in that manner it stood there before the door, being water to

them for their comfort, and yet not water to invade the place."

Which is a pretty impressive miracle!

**San Zeno rock**

Inside the church, sitting in a corner is the San Zeno rock.

San Zeno used to sit on it when fishing in the Adige. It has come to symbolise the belief that Saint Zeno was a fisher-of-men. It sits on top of a conveniently sized Roman funeral monument which has a bust of a husband and wife on it – it has nothing to do with Zeno at all.

There are also some other ancient frescoes to be seen and a statue of San Zeno himself.

*Map 8.4 - When you exit the church turn left to walk to a T-junction.*

*Turn left into Stradone Antonio Provolo to reach the walls of Castelvecchio once more.*

*Map 8.5 - Turn right to back uphill and return to the main road.*

*When you get there, turn left to return to the Ponte di Castelvecchio Archway.*

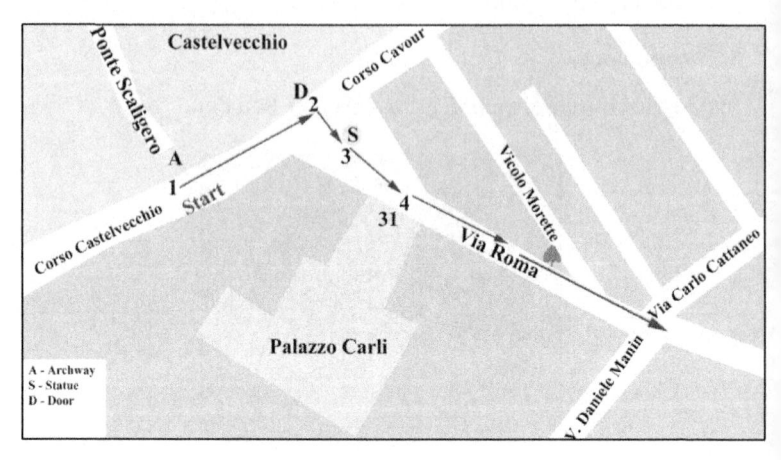

Map 9

## Back into Town

*Map 9.1 - With the Archway behind you, turn left and walk to the main door of the Castelvecchio Museum.*

*Map 9.2 - Opposite the museum is a square where you will find a statue of Camillo Benso Conti di Cavour. Cross over to reach it.*

## Camillo Benso Conte di Cavour

Cavour gets a statue because he was one of the leaders in the battle for Italian Unification. In fact he supplied the political brainpower and savvy to achieve Italian Independence when the fighting failed.

Once most of Italy was united as one country a prime minister was needed, and Cavour was the first to fill that role. He died after a few months and sadly didn't see Rome and Venice join. The long street you have just walked down is named after him.

*Mao 9.3 - Standing face to face with Cavour, walk straight ahead into Via Roma.*

*This curving road will take you towards Piazza Bra. Pause at the Palazzo Carli at number 31 on your right.*

## Palazzo Carli

This palace started as a private residence but was later sold to the Austrian Hungarian Empire who used it to house various important military personnel. It was here that Austria finally signed Verona away in 1866, letting Verona become part of a United Italy.

The Palace stayed in military hands and even today it's the seat of the Italian Army Operational Land Forces Command.

It has an interesting inscription above the door "Satis Beatus" which translates as "Happy Enough".

*Map 9.4 - Continue along Via Roma, crossing a junction with Via Carlo Cattaneo and Via Daniele Manin.*

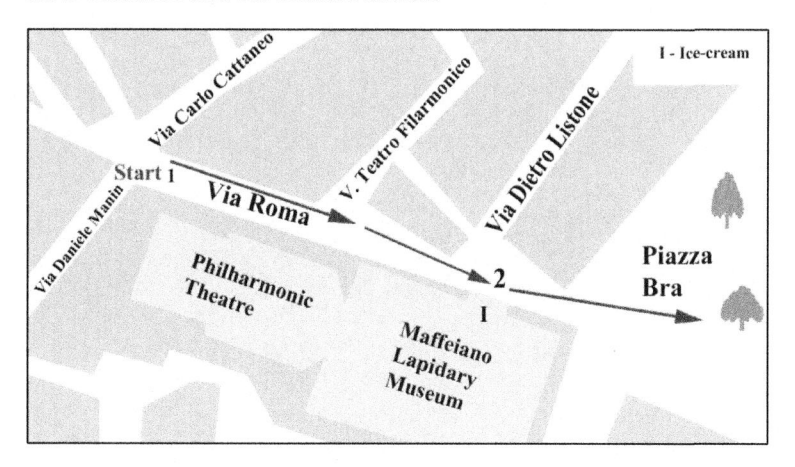

Map 10

*Map 10.1 – Continue along Via Roma and you will eventually reach a large many-columned building on your right.*

That is the Maffeiano Lapidary Museum which you might already have visited on Walk 1.

## Ice-cream

If an ice-cream appeals there is a very good gelateria here which you might already have visited after walk 1. Gelateria Savoia sits behind the columns on your right at number 1B.

*Map 10.2 - With or without an ice-cream continue along Via Roma a few more steps to return to Piazza Bra.*

You have now reached the end of this walk.

# Walk 5 – Across the River

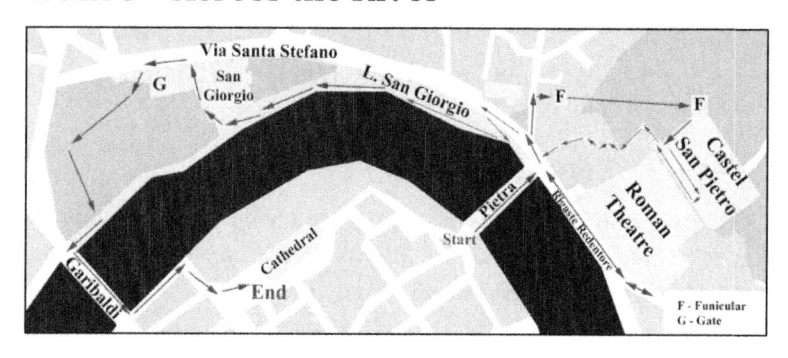

Overview Walk 5

This walk takes you across the river to visit the Roman Theatre followed by a cable car ride up to the castle viewpoint.

You then descend the hill and walk along the river before re-crossing the river to finish at the cathedral.

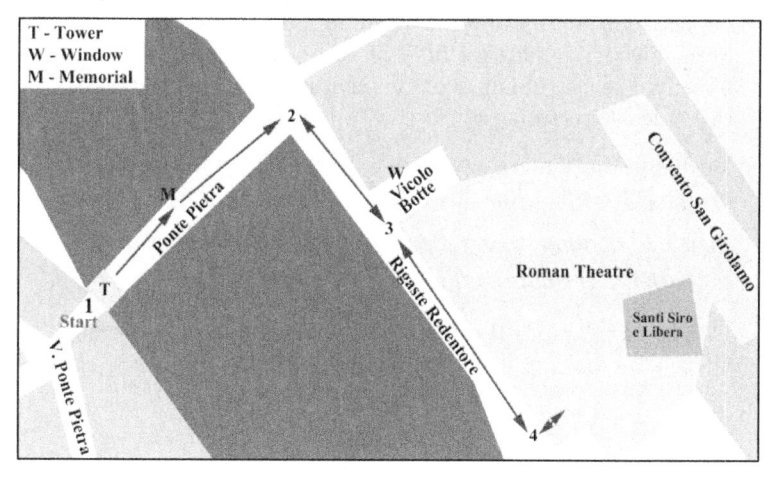

Map 1

This walk starts on Via Ponte Pietra which you may have already seen on walk 3.

*Map 1.1 - Start at the tower and archway which give access to the Ponte Pietra. Go through the archway and onto the bridge.*

You can read about the Ponte Pietra on Page 86 if you haven't tackled Walk 3.

## Over the Ponte Pietra

*Map 1.2 – Cross to the other side of the bridge. Then turn right to walk along the riverside on Rigaste Redentore. Pause at little Vicolo Botte, it's the first street on your left.*

## Vicolo Botte

In Vicolo Botte on the left-hand side there is a fascinating little window which looks like a face with a very wide mouth.

## View of the bridge

From the riverside you will get the best view of the bridge.

The two arches on the right are the only survivors from Roman Times – they are built of white stone. The other arches have had to be rebuilt over the centuries and they are made of rather less interesting brick.

At one time there was a matching tower on this side of the bridge but it was taken down in the nineteenth century.

*Map 1.3 - Continue along the riverside passing a hedge on your left to reach the entrance to the Roman Theatre.*

You can explore the Roman Theatre, the old church of Santi Siro e Libera, and the Archaeological Museum.

## Roman Theatre

The theatre was built in the 1st century BC when Augustus was Emperor. At that time the theatre was topped by a magnificent temple. However this area of Verona was abandoned when Rome fell, and after centuries of neglect the theatre disappeared beneath buildings and huts which were constructed on top of it.

The theatre was rediscovered in the eighteenth century, when Andrea Monga, a very rich merchant, bought some of those buildings specifically so he could begin archaeological excavations. In 1904 Verona stepped in and took over the entire site. The remaining buildings which had been placed on top of the theatre were removed as part of the project to restore it.

So what we have today is the stage, the orchestra pit in front of and below the stage, and stone seating where you can sit to take it all in. Look into the orchestra pit and spot the square stones with holes in the middle. They were used to control ropes which were pulled to open and close the curtains of the stage

Face away from the stage and look diagonally right to spot the church of Santi Siro e Libera, one of the many religious buildings which once covered this area.

## Chiesa dei Santi Siro e Libera

It was built in the 10th century although it has also been through a later remodeling. It's dedicated to Saint Siro, who was the boy who gave Jesus five loaves and two fish which Jesus turned into a feast for the multitudes. Siro became Christian and travelled to Verona preaching the gospel and became a Saint.

Climb its unusual steep double stairway to enter.

As you reach the porch look under the arch to see the inscription which states that Saint Siro celebrated the first mass in Verona near this spot. Inside the church you will find a beautiful white altar decorated with a host of cherubs and a wonderful white marble curtain cascading around the altarpiece.

## Archaeological Museum

The museum is in an old monastery dedicated to Saint Jerome. In it you will find many Roman treasures from Verona and its surrounding areas. Take your time to wander through the complex, and enjoy the ancient sculptures, mosaics etc.

Descend to the basement into the Inscriptions Room where you will find the colourful mosaic which was discovered in Piazza Bra – we see Bacchus, the god of wine accompanied by panthers. Don't miss going into the cloister to find Roman tombstones and statues, and along the terrace for yet more statues and views.

***Map 1.4 - When you exit the theatre complex, turn right to walk back along the riverside and return to the Stone Bridge.***

As you do, spot the circular window and arched window on the arches of the bridge. The theory is that if the water level rose to that height the openings would alleviate some of the pressure by letting some of the water pass through.

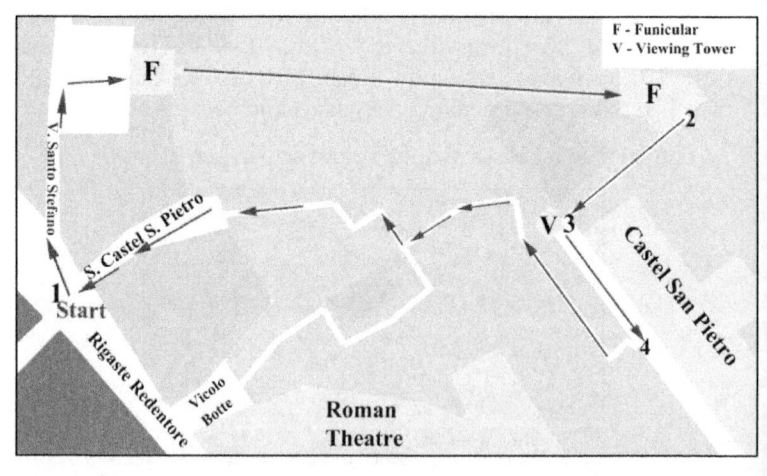

Map 2

***Map 2.1 - Walk past the bridge. You will soon reach a fork in the road. Take the right hand road, Via Santo Stefano.***

*You will find the funicular on your right. Buy a ticket and sail up to the top.*

## From the Funicular

*Map 2.2 - When you exit the funicular station, follow the walkway to a viewing platform.*

You are at one of the best viewing points in the city.

Below you the Adige makes a wind curve, and is a pretty sight with the old town behind it. Spot the cathedral and its tower, which is where this walk ends.

*Map 2.3 - Leave the viewing platform and follow the walkway right. The Castel San Pietro will be on your left.*

## Colle San Pietro

The hill you are standing on is called Saint Peter's hill, and it is actually the oldest part of Verona. It's named after the local Saint Peter you might have read about earlier on Walk 3, not the apostle.

The experts tell us that people have lived on this hill since the 6th century BC. The historians think the name Verona comes from the Etruscan verone, which means terrace and refers to the terraces you are now standing on.

When the Romans arrived, they shifted the centre of town over the river, to where it is flat and where they could build following the standard Roman grid pattern. They still made use of the hill though, placing temples and the theatre in dramatic settings overlooking the town.

## Castel San Pietro

There has always been a defensive castle on this hill since Roman times, but the one you see behind you is obviously not Roman. It was built by the Austrians in the nineteenth century as a barracks, and if needed the soldiers could bombard the city below – a means of keeping the locals in order. It has lain empty and unloved for many years, but there are moves afoot to turn it into a museum.

*Map 2.4 - When you have had enough of the view, find the stairway from the terrace which will take you back down to the riverside.*

*Always keep to the main path and right-hand side as you descend. You should eventually find yourself back at the Stone Bridge.*

*If you do take a wrong turn, then when you reach the riverside just look along it to find the Stone Bridge and make your way back to it.*

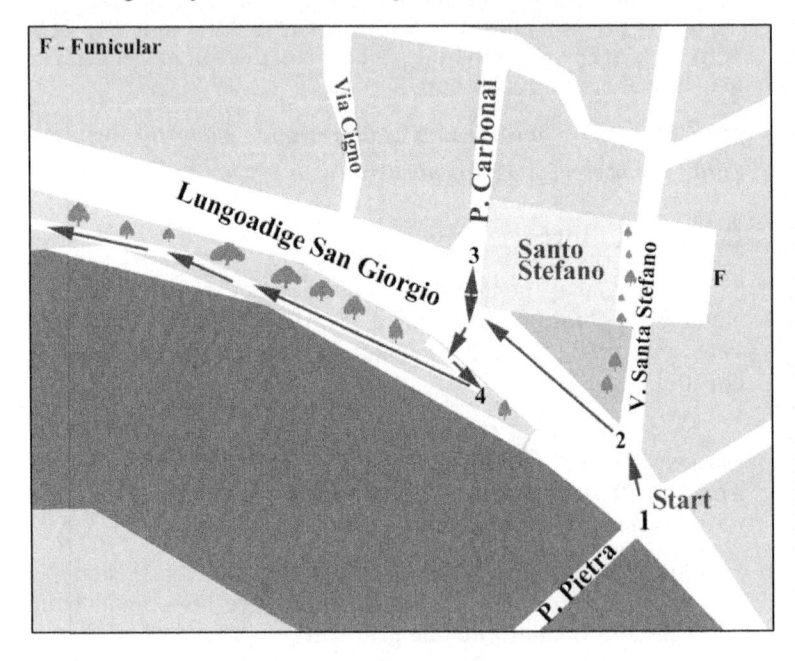

Map 3

The remainder of this walk is a pleasant stroll along the riverside, seeing a few more churches and Roman remains, before crossing the Ponte Garibaldi to return to Cathedral square.

If that doesn't appeal or if you are short on time, just re-cross the Ponte Pietra here to return to finish the walk.

Otherwise -

*Map 3.1 - With the Stone Bridge in front of you, turn right to walk along the river side.*

*Map 3.2 - When you reach the fork in the road, this time take the left hand road, Lungoadige San Giorgio.*

**On your right you will see the church of Santo Stefano. Don't miss its lovely octagonal bell-tower.**

**Keep walking along the riverside to reach the far side of the church, as that is where the entrance is.**

## Santo Stefano

A Roman temple to Isis once stood here, but in the fifth century the remains of Saint Stephen were found in what is now Israel. He is said to have been the first Christian martyr and was stoned outside Jerusalem. Churches dedicated to him sprung up all over Europe including here in Verona.

Verona's first church to Saint Stephen was built here over the old temple to Isis, and in fact some of the stones of the temple are built into the church. It burned down a few times over the centuries but was always rebuilt. Some historians think it was used as Verona's cathedral up to the 10th century.

### Varalli Chapel

The church's highlight is the ornate Varalli Chapel which is on your right as you go in the main door. It was built to house the relics brought up from the crypt, including those of Verona's early bishops, and of forty martyrs from Verona who were murdered by Emperor Diocletian.

More in legend than fact, it's also believed that the chapel is home to the relics of children murdered during Herod's massacre of the Innocents – when he ordered the murder of all the Jewish baby boys in an attempt to get rid of Jesus. Because of that the chapel is also called The Chapel of the Innocents.

The paintings in the chapel commemorate all three events; on the left you can see The Forty Martyrs, in the centre The Massacre of the Innocents, and on the right The Five Holy Bishops.

**The Cathedra**

As you explore the church you will find a rather simple stone chair. It's thought to be a cathedra – a chair used by the bishop when he was in the church. This one is very simple and plain as it comes from the eighth century. Bishop's chairs are usually much grander golden affairs.

**The Crypt**

Two sets of stairs give you access to the crypt. The crypt itself is a forest of columns and a wonderful ceiling decorated with lilies and foliage. The columns are made of either red Verona marble, or a dark grey stone called syenite which comes from Egypt – so it's believed those columns were from the temple to Isis. Behind the altar stands a statue of Saint Stephen and some colourful frescoes, including another depiction of the Massacre of the Innocents.

*Map 3.3 - When you exit the church, cross the road to reach the railing. Turn left to descend the steps down to the riverside.*

*Map 3.4 - Turn right to walk along the riverside.*

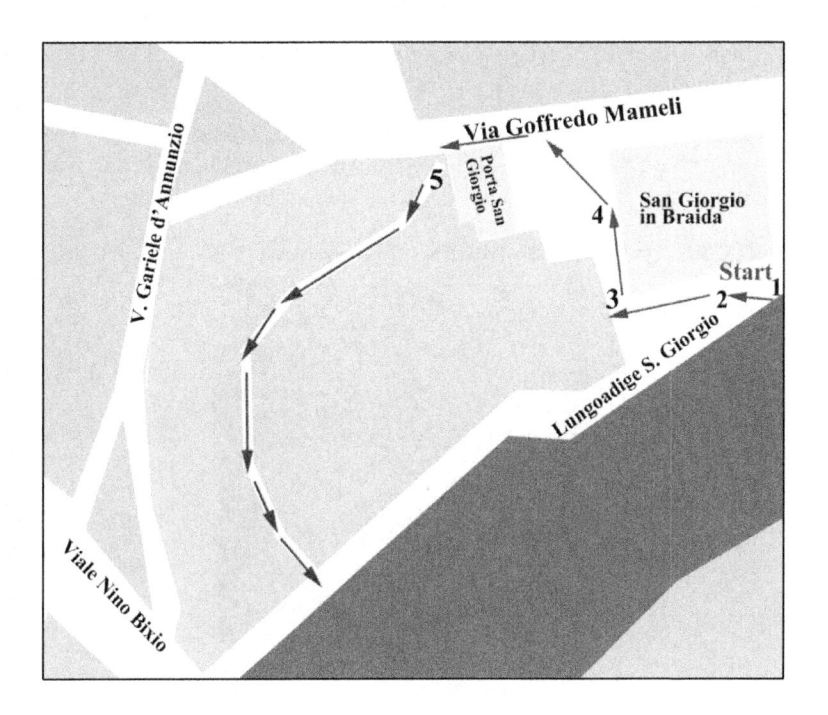

Map 4

*Map 4.1 - After a five minute riverside stroll, you will reach some more steps which will take you back up to the walkway and the San Giorgio in Barida church.*

*Map 4.2 - Continue along the riverside, and once past the church you will you see a walled garden.*

*Map 4.3 - Turn right just before the garden to approach the front of San Giorgio in Braida which sits on a square.*

## San Giorgio in Braida

This church was built over an old eleventh century Benedictine monastery, but the bell-tower is all that is left of it. The church did have another tower but it was lopped off and replaced by a dome as fashions changed. Michele Sanmicheli was the architect in charge – you have already seen some of his other buildings on other walks.

The church is worth visiting to see its works of art. The German poet Goethe visited Verona when he was in Italy, and was so impressed that he called the church a "splendid art gallery".

**The Martyrdom of Saint George - Veronese**

The most famous painting in the church hangs over the man altar. This is one of the many works of art which Napoleon had shipped to Paris in the eighteenth century. It was returned to Verona in 1815.

Saint George is about to be killed because he refused to give up his Christianity. The hooded man behind him is pointing to a statue of Apollo and insisting that he worship it. Saint George is having none of it and looks up to the heavens where various saints and The Virgin Mary are watching. The little cherub which is in the centre of the painting is carrying a palm wreath to Saint George which indicates he is about to become a martyr.

Another Veronese painting called the Miracle of Saint Barnabas was also lifted by Napoleon but it remains in France, in Rouen. You can see a copy of it near the choir.

*Map 4.4 - When you leave the church, face away from the front of the church, and in front of you stands the back of Porta San Giorgio with its three archways.*

*Walk around its right-hand side to reach the side visitors to Verona would have seen as they entered the city.*

## Porta San Giorgio

It was built into the town wall by Cangrande 1 and if you look left and right you can see the town wall stretching away, and what remains of the moat beneath you. The main door of the gate had a drawbridge across it.

The gate is thought by many to be the most elegant in Verona. Its design was inspired by the Arco dei Gavi which you will have seen on walk 4.

*Map 4.5 - There are a few steps leading up to a pathway next to the gate. The pathway crosses a little park called Parco Cesare Lombroso. Follow the path, keeping the moat on your left all the way back to the riverside.*

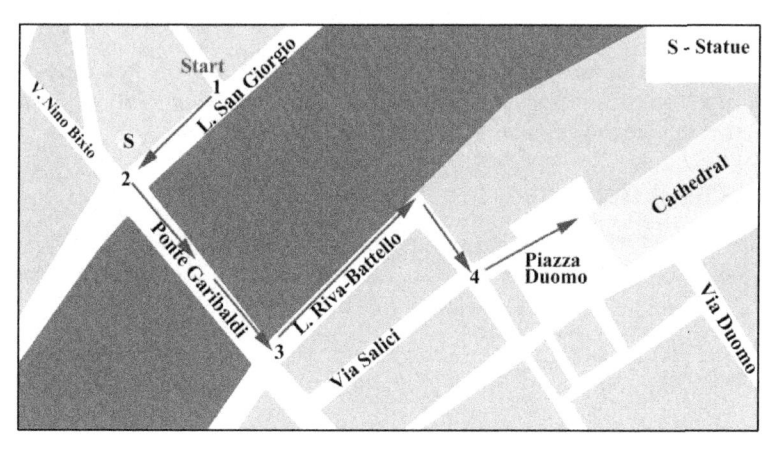

Map 5

*Map 5.1 - Once you reach the riverside, turn right to reach the next bridge. Before you cross it take a look at the statue in the park on your right.*

## Cesare Lombroso

The park you just walked through is named after Cesare Lombroso and this is his statue. He was born in Verona in the nineteenth century and he studied at some of Europe's best universities.

He is known for his "Born Criminal" theory which is definitely no longer deemed acceptable. His theories, which were accepted and followed at the time, stated that criminals were a throwback to an earlier type of human, and that criminals could be identified by physical features such as a low forehead, ear size and even arm length.

*Now turn your attention to the bridge.*

## Ponte Garibaldi

There have been several bridges here. The first bridge was named after Giuseppe Garibaldi once Verona had joined Italy.

It has been destroyed or damaged a few times, the last time by the retreating German army. It has always been rebuilt. This bridge was re-opened in 1947 and so far has survived intact.

## The Witches

This bridge was blown up during the German retreat. It was originally decorated with four statues called The Strachi (The Witches), but they were lost in the devastation.

Verona searched the riverbed for the marble pieces after the war, but only one called The Mother was found. At the time of writing it is being restored.

There has been a lot of talk about re-sculpting the group of statues and replacing them on the bridge. So perhaps you will be able to enjoy the Witches as you cross.

*Map 5.2 – Cross the bridge.*

*Map 5.3 - Once over turn left into Lungadige Riva-Battell. Walk along the riverside until you have to turn right into Vicolo San Girolamo.*

*Map 5.4 - You will reach a crossroads. Turn left, staying on Vicolo San Girolamo, to reach the Cathedral Square where this walk ends.*

# Walk 6 - Juliet's Tomb?

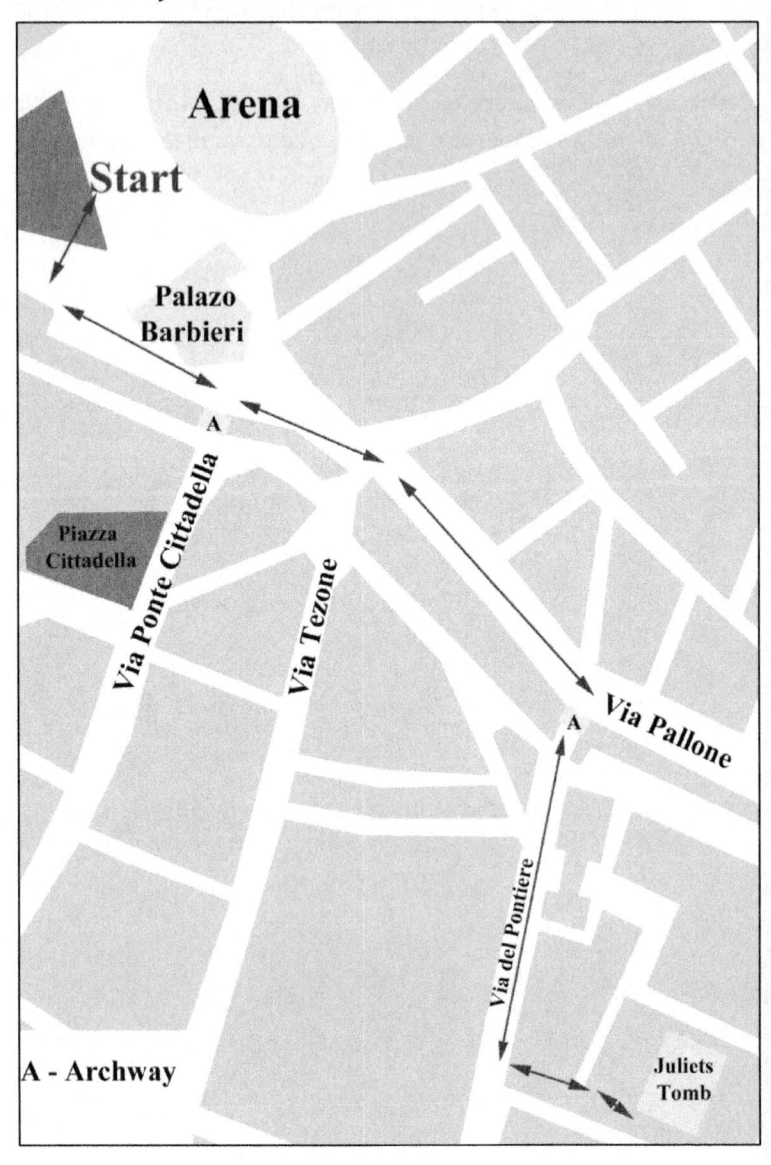

Overview Walk 6

This walk takes you a little off the beaten track. It will take you ten minutes walking to get to Juliet's Tomb, and ten minutes to get back.

Well of course it's not really her tomb, but according to Shakespeare the lovers were buried in a Franciscan monastery which sat outside Verona's wall, and the San Francesco al Corso monastery fits the bill.

In 1937 the Director of Veronese Museums, Antonio Avena, decided to make use of that important fact. A handy ancient sarcophagus, which had lain empty in the monastery for centuries, was deemed the ideal prop and declared as the tomb of Juliet.

Note, the entrance price includes a visit to a little fresco museum in the same monastery, which justifies the price they are charging to see the "tomb".

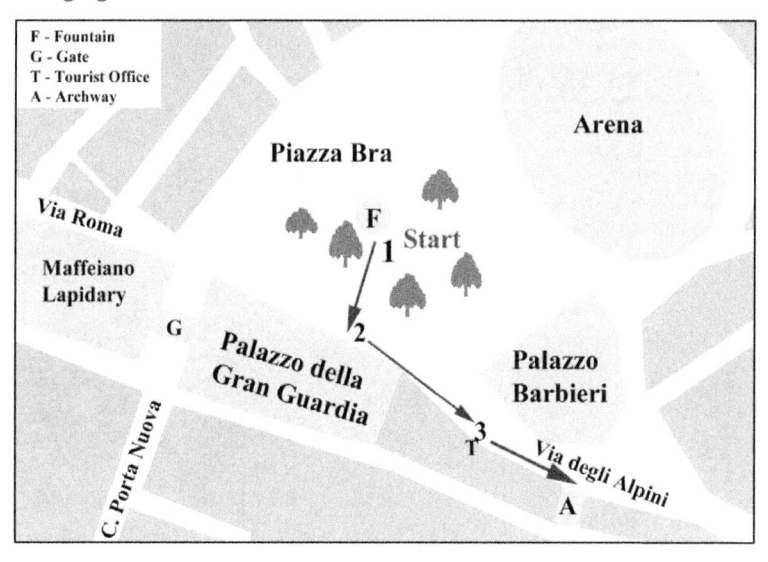

Map 1

This walk starts in Piazza Bra. Start at the fountain which sits in the middle of the square.

*Map 1.1 – Face away from the Arena and walk over to the Palazzo della Gran Guardia which sits at the top of some steps.*

*Map 1.2 – Turn left to walk along Via degli Alpini, passing the tourist office as you do.*

*Mao 1.3 - Follow the city wall, passing a series of doors on your right before reaching the archway of Porta Cittadella.*

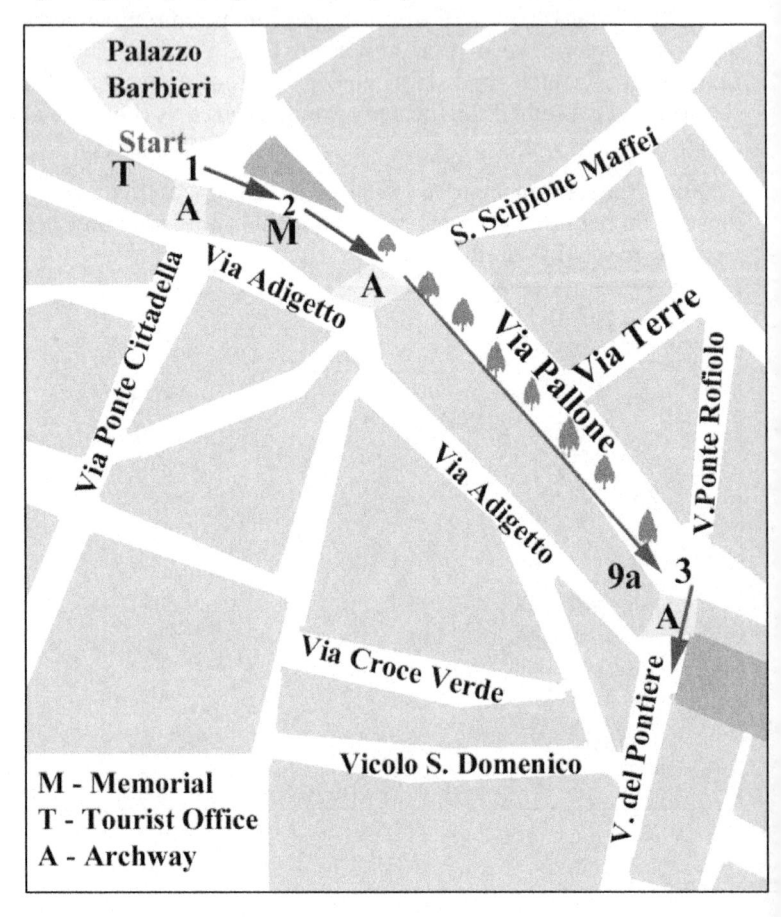

Map 2

*Map 2.1 – Stay outside the wall. Once you pass the Porta Cittadella you will find another war memorial on your right. Keep going!*

*Map 2.2 - Some trees on your left will give you some shade as the road bends to the right. You will pass several doors in the wall and some small archways as you do. The doors are numbered, so continue to reach number 9a.*

*A few more steps will bring you to a large archway which has a tower on its right-hand side. A road runs through the archway.*

*Map 2.3 - Turn right through the archway onto Via del Pontiere – you can find the street name under the archway on its left-side.*

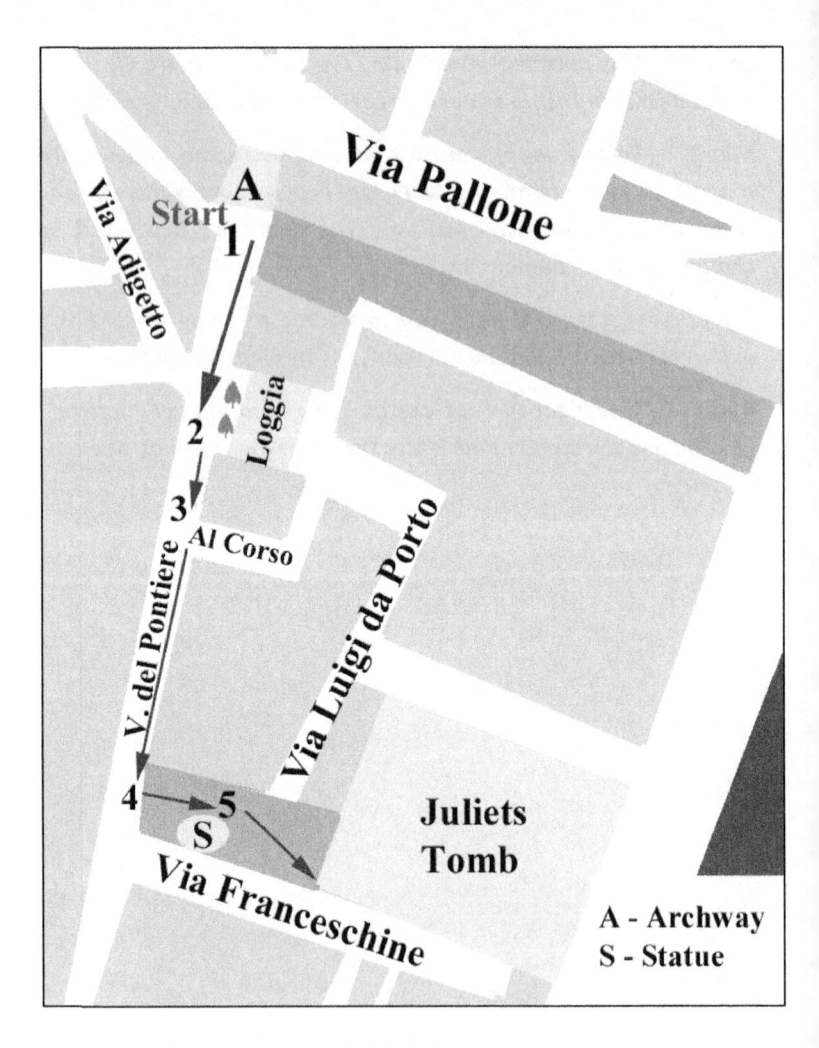

Map 3

*Map 3.1 - Once through the archway walk straight ahead to follow Via Pontiere. You will reach a pretty loggia which is fronted by two little trees on your left-hand side.*

*Map 3.2 - Continue straight ahead and pass narrow Vicolo S. Francesco Al Corso on your left.*

*Map 3.3 - Walk past one more block to reach a green area on your left – nearly there.*

*Map 3.4 - You will see a path leading across the lawn and it is bordered by trees. Follow the path and near its start you will find the statue of Liang Shanbo and Zhu Yintai.*

## Liang Shanbo and Zhu Yingtai

It celebrates a Chinese romantic tragedy which is sometimes called China's Romeo and Juliet.

Zhu was the only daughter of a wealthy family. With the permission of her father she attended college but went disguised as a boy, since of course girls in general were not educated – sounds very Shakespearean already.

She became great friends and then fell in love with another student called Liang, but bookworm Liang didn't realise that his new best buddy Zhu was a girl.

Zhu was called back home and Liang promised to visit. When he did he made the startling discovery and realised that he loved Zhu. As you have probably guessed Zhu's parents had already arranged a suitable marriage and it was not to Liang. Liang was devastated and died of grief.

On Zhu's wedding day she visited Liang's grave. She begged the grave to open. The skies thundered and the grave opened. Zhu threw herself into it and the two spirits merged into a pair of beautiful butterflies who flew away together.

That's a happier ending than poor old Romeo and Juliet.

*Map 3.5 - Walk along the path to the end of the little green area. You will find the entrance to the monastery and Juliet's Tomb in the right-hand corner.*

## Juliet's Tomb

Once you enter the monastery grounds make your way around the cloister – it has a lovely old well in the middle.

Follow the signs to reach the stairs down to the crypt.

Just before you descend spot the wall plaque with the words of the bard:

> A grave? O No; a lantern..
> for here lies Juliet, and her beauty makes
> this vault a feasting presence of light

You will descend to a very ancient chamber where "Juliet's tomb" lies; her sarcophagus is made of red Verona marble. This is supposed to be the spot where Juliet killed herself believing that Romeo was dead.

It's not as popular as Juliet's house, as it does take more of an effort to reach it, but it's probably more atmospheric because of the lack of crowds.

## Dickens

Charles Dickens visited and he wrote in his "Pictures of Italy":

> "So, I went off, with a guide, to an old, old garden, once belonging to an old, old, convent, I suppose; and being admitted, at a shattered gate, by a bright-eyed woman who was washing clothes, went down some walks where fresh plants and young flowers were prettily growing among fragments of old wall, and ivy-coloured mounds; and was shown a little tank, or water-trough, which the bright-eyed woman called "La tomba di Giulietta la sfortunàta" (the tomb of Juliet the unfortunate).
>
> With the best disposition in the world to believe, I could do no more than believe that the bright-eyed woman believed. It is better for Juliet to lie out of the track of tourists, and to have no visitors but such as come to graves in spring-rain, and sweet air, and sunshine."

There is also a series of small bronze plaques on display. They are by Sergio Pasetto who did the bust of Shakespeare on Piazza Bra. You will see replicas of some of the plaques as you explore Verona. They are placed at the assumed locations of key scenes of Romeo and Juliet.

To be honest it won't take you very long to see the tomb, take a snap, and wonder what to do next. Well make your way back upstairs to the cloister, and then find the door to the fresco museum. It's small but it is worth a look.

## Fresco Museum

The museum stands on the site of an old monastery/convent which over the centuries was used by orders of monks and nuns.

Napoleon dissolved the monasteries/convents during his short reign and this building ended up being used by his army. After his defeat it returned to a more charitable role in housing the poor. It was then badly damaged in World War II, but thankfully Italy had started to care for its ancient heritage, saved it, and turned it into this museum.

Modern life has destroyed much of Verona's painted decoration but this museum keeps many surviving treasures.

You will find fragments of twelfth century frescoes saved from the Sacellum of San Michele. It was an ancient complex of cellars used for worship which were discovered under the church of San Nazaro and Celso in Verona. Those frescoes were carefully removed and placed in this museum.

Interestingly their removal revealed an even older set of frescoes in the Sacellum which have been left in place.

There are some beautiful fragments to look at in the museum.

The above fresco's subject has some beautiful beadwork woven into her hair.

Other frescoes are from a later period and are much more complete. They have been taken from the facades and interiors of Verona's palazzos.

There is one long fresco showing Charles V and Pope Clement VII riding to the coronation of Charles V as Holy Roman Emperor. The Pope and the King are the two wearing ornate golden cloaks under a canopy - the King has the double headed eagle of Austria on his cloak. He ruled vast swathes of Europe and spoke many languages. He is quoted as stating:

> "I speak Spanish to God, Italian to women,
> French to men, and German to my horse"

Much more fun are the two horses further back in the procession shown above. They are very lively and seem to be looking out towards at you.

There are also some frescoes depicting stories from Greek mythology – including poor Marsyas who was flayed alive for the sin of challenging the God Apollo to a flute contest.

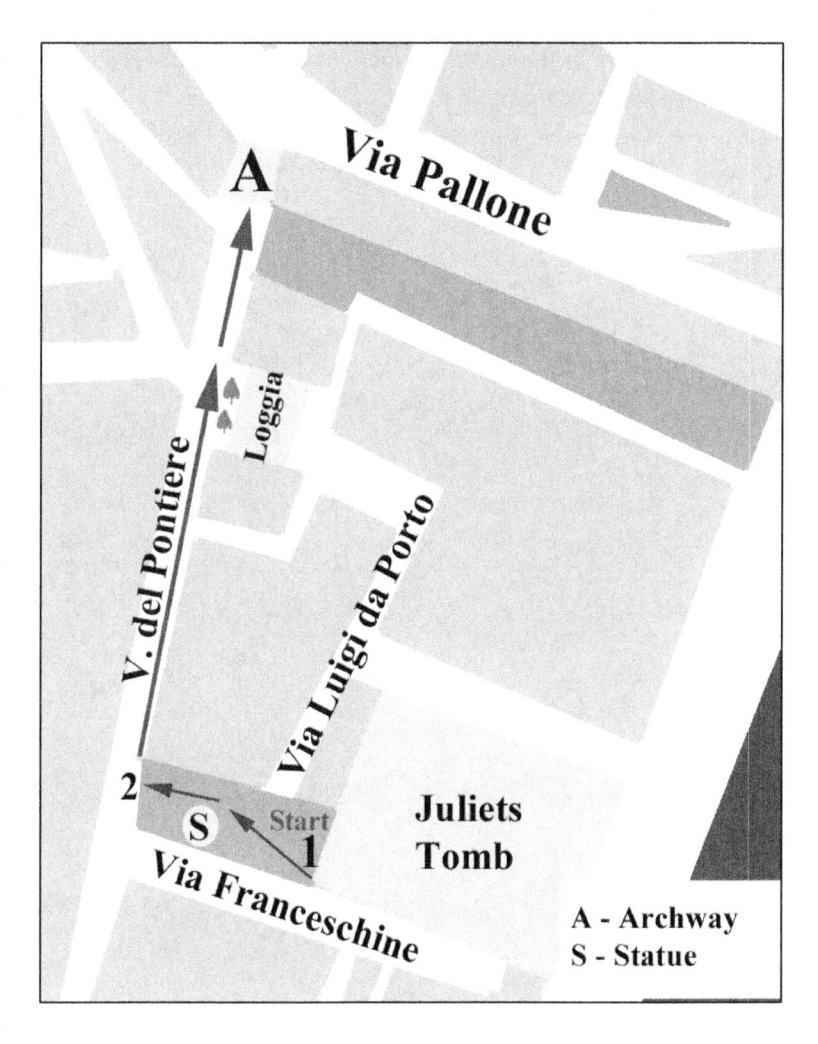

Map 4

When you have seen enough frescoes it's time to backtrack to the Arena.

***Map 4.1 - To do so, exit the monastery and walk along the path across the little lawn passing Liang Shanbo and Zhu Yingtai.***

*Map 4.2 - Turn right onto Via Pontiere and follow it until you reach the town wall archway once more.*

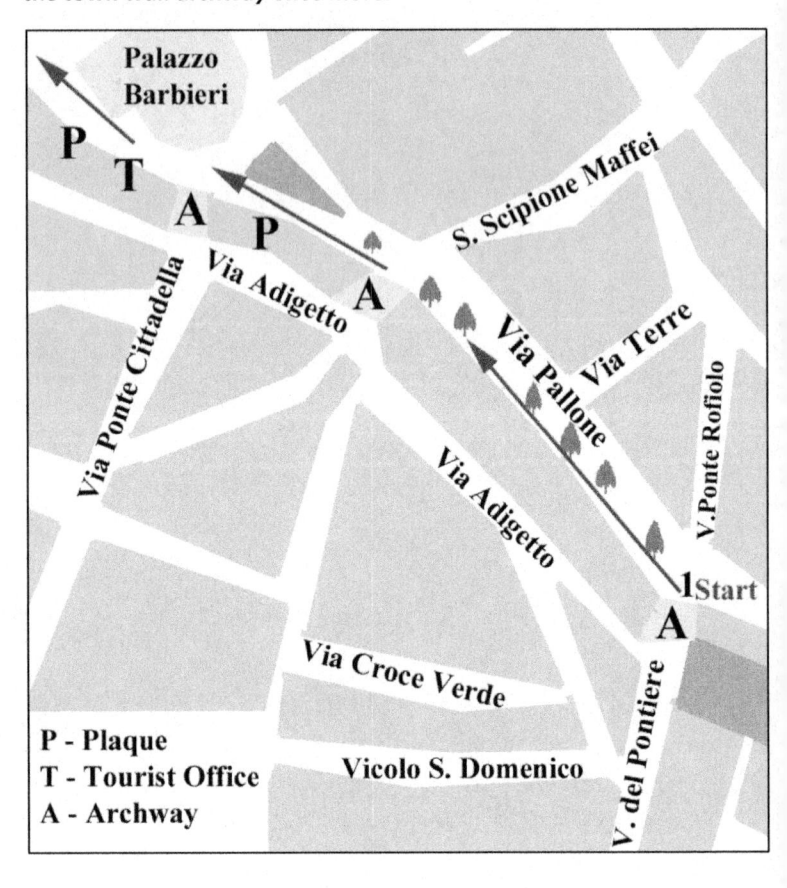

Map 5

*Map 4.3 - Go through the archway and turn left. Follow the city wall all the way back to Palazzo Bra.*

# Did you enjoy these walks?

I do hope you found these walks both fun and interesting, and I would love feedback, so please review this book

You could also drop me a line on my amazon web page.

## Other Strolling Around Books to try:

- Strolling Around Antwerp
- Strolling Around Amsterdam
- Strolling Around Arles
- Strolling Around Bath
- Strolling Around Berlin
- Strolling Around Bilbao
- Strolling Around Bruges
- Strolling Around Delft
- Strolling Around Florence
- Strolling Around Ghent
- Strolling Around Jerez
- Strolling Around Lisbon
- Strolling Around Ljubljana
- Strolling Around Lucca
- Strolling Around Madrid
- Strolling Around Palma
- Strolling Around Pisa
- Strolling Around Porto
- Strolling Around Sienna
- Strolling Around The Hague
- Strolling Around Toledo

Printed in Great Britain
by Amazon